# HACKING FOR AGILE CHANGE

## with an agile mindset, behaviours & practices

LENA ROSS

**Disclaimer**

The information in this book is designed to provide helpful information on the subjects discussed, and the material does not represent professional advice. The author disclaims any liability to any person arising directly or indirectly from the use of, or for any errors or omissions, the information contained in this book. The adoption and application of the information in this book is at the reader's discretion and is his or her sole responsibility.

Title: Hacking for Agile Change: with an agile mindset, behaviours and practices

Author: Lena Ross



ISBN: 978-0-6481017-4-1

Cover design: Amelia Lazarus, Jonathan Vu, Alana Nanasca and Sigitjaka Nakula

Photographer: Joanne Rinaldi

Typesetting: Green Hill Publishing

First print: 2017

# CONTENTS

# PREFACE

Back in 2007, I was fortunate to start a role at one of the Australian 'big four' banks as a Change Manager in a progressive division that was establishing a 'change practice'. At that time, whilst change management as a profession wasn't entirely new, it was an occupation that was still being defined in terms of capabilities and deliverables. This gave me a tremendous opportunity to be part of a team, with experienced and insightful colleagues. Together, we shaped what a change centre of excellence could look like, to help our senior stakeholders who were the change leaders in our business, to appreciate the value of having dedicated change practitioners on board as permanent employees.

In the early phases, we needed more clarity in our roles when working on projects, often with project managers who were unclear about what value change practitioners could bring. This ambiguity indicated that the time was right to more clearly define our roles, our skills and most importantly, our value proposition.

With a background in learning and organisational development, in this first role with an official change manager title, I offered to draft the bank's first competency framework for our change practitioners. The objective was to help us define our core competencies and position our service offerings to our business. This early draft was adopted by other divisions and formed the foundations for the enterprise change capability framework that is still used today in this organisation. Whilst the framework has been refreshed, it continues to inform capability assessments, role descriptions at each change capability level, career and development planning, and resourcing and recruitment decisions.

Being there in the foundational phase meant we could experiment with different methodologies and approaches, to find out what worked well to shape a change framework. At the same time, with the bank recognising the value of having in-house change resources, our team members were often asked to run sessions for senior leaders on change leadership to help build organisational capability.

Fast forward to 2013: it's organisational realignment time. It was apparent that it was sound business sense to 'converge' the disparate change practices and methods from each division, to form a true Enterprise Change Practice. With the uncertainty and disruption of this major organisational restructure came many potential opportunities for those who stayed on. As serendipity had it, my own capabilities and background were needed to help shape this centralised change practice to define the capabilities and to establish and embed a scalable enterprise-wide change framework. Along with loads of hard work came more opportunities to experiment, co-create and engage with a range of wonderful people inside and outside the organisation to make a difference.

By the end of 2015, we had established ourselves as a highly regarded change practice within the organisation and in the industry. During my time in the Enterprise Change Practice, I was invited to speak at industry networking events about our change framework, along with emerging insights such as the human hardwired responses to change. At the same time, I was also being asked to 'guest blog' about some of the initiatives we implemented. The icing on the cake came just before I left the bank at the end of 2015 with industry accolades. Leveraging the concept of social learning, I developed and implemented the NED (Nimble Education Delivery) talks (modelled on the successful TED talks) which won the inaugural award in the new category of Social and Collaborative Learning at the Australian Institute of Training (AITD) Excellence Awards.

After years of being fascinated with human behaviour, overlaid by these eight great years of working at the bank in a time when change was being further defined and acknowledged as a practice in its own right, I've finally decided to review what's worked and compile the 'must-knows' for all involved in the 'change value chain' across an organisation. My experience has been enriched by engagement with change leaders and sponsors, the people who initiate change, the project team members, human resources professionals, the people receiving the change, and of course the dedicated change practitioners. The tips and hacks in this book are designed to keep people productive, inspired and engaged as we embrace disruptive, relentless change together. The proven approaches consider techniques for co-creation and deeper engagement.

So the time has come to do just that! In the spirit of working out loud, along with social learning and collaboration, it's time to share what I've learned, researched and applied, with like-minded folk like you. Here I am taking the plunge and putting myself out there with this book. Our working lives - and our personal lives - are filled with disruption and new ways of working for you to be curious about. And I hope you can pick up a hack or two that is helpful, or at least to provoke your thinking.

## WHY THIS BOOK IS DIFFERENT

This book will cover *what* has worked, *when* it's worked, and more importantly, *how* it worked. It will explain things they *don't* tell you in change management courses. It will share real experiences on how the rubber hits the ground and what to look out for. It details *how* things were done and *when* the activities can be applied.

It will help you understand what you can do, as a change leader, a change practitioner and project manager, when you are asked to support an 'agile' project; and even when you are not asked, you will have ideas and examples so you can introduce agile practices to any change initiative to more deeply engage your stakeholders.

*There is a strong focus on the people side of change.*

We know that change itself is changing, relentlessly and continuously. Fewer CEOs are sponsoring long-term, multi-year transformation programmes. Shorter, faster iterations are demanding a refresh of change management capabilities and the need to rethink our approach to how we deliver change.

The change practitioner's capability toolkit is expanding. Typically, change practitioners will find themselves landing in more projects using agile practices. Change frameworks are quickly adjusting to align to this way of delivery. With agile change practices fast becoming part of the change leader and practitioner toolkit, we also need to adopt agility in our behaviours and thinking.

We know the word 'agile' is used almost everywhere. Recruiters are asking for *agile* experience because employers want *agile* people. Organisations want to be *agile*. *Agile* is interpreted as many things and needs to be defined so we can understand it better. In order to make sense of what 'agile' means in a context that is broader than just what we do, we need to define it as a capability.

### *'Agile' as an organisational capability*

Agility is so much more than a software development approach or a project methodology. It's a mindset, along with a set of behaviours and practices. So what does agility look like in practice? How do we make sense of agility? Defining agile as a capability demystifies the word itself, and helps us understand what it actually means for individuals, teams and organisations.

To explain this, I've developed this pyramid model that shows the layers of agile as a capability. At the base is the fourth layer, *organisational agility*.

For an organisation to become agile, it needs people with capability in each of these parts: people who are agile in their thinking, their actions and in their practices.

To explore these elements in greater detail, this book is divided into the three parts that support organisational capability:

**1** | How you think

**2** | How you act

**3** | What you do and deliver.

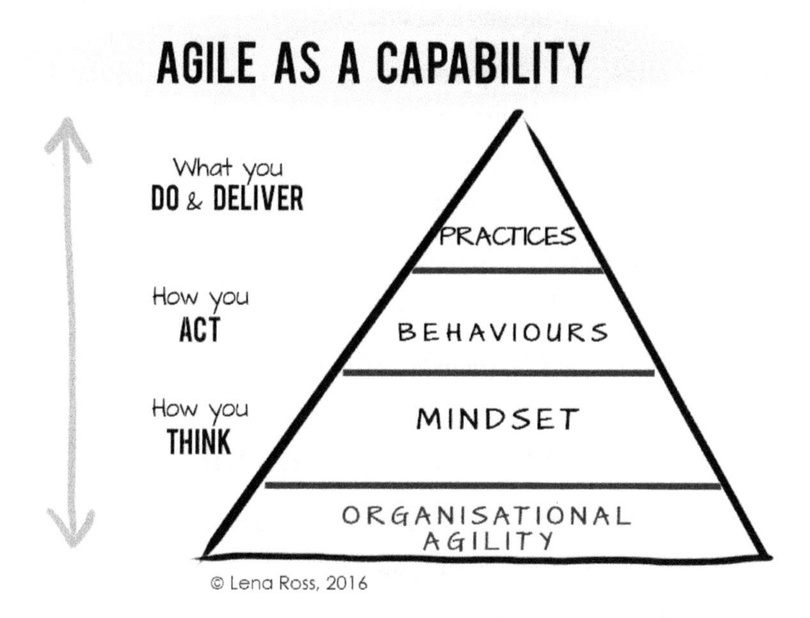


### *1. Agile mindset - how you THINK*

Throughout the book, there will be numerous references to *agile* and *lean* practices, but it's not exclusively about agile project application. Being truly agile starts with an agility in mindset. Such a mindset is open to learning and trying new things, is comfortable with uncertainty, is intensely curious, dares to experiment and is not frightened to fail.

### *2. Agile behaviours - how you ACT*

Agile behaviours, at team or individual level, can be broadly described as behaviours that rely on collaboration, transparency, honesty, willingness to work outside the team or individual's area of expertise, and where the team or individual is adaptable and open to feedback so they can continuously improve their practices.

### *3. Agile practice - what you DO and DELIVER*

There are numerous agile practices that work best when the team members demonstrate agile behaviours and mindset. Of course, you don't need to be working on a project that's officially declared 'agile' to apply agile practices such as stand-up meetings and Kanban boards.

The next chapter explores 'agile' as a word and a framework, as well as its application and its place in an organisation.

Simply put, to be agile is a *mindset* AND a *skill set.*

## OTHER CONSIDERATIONS

The chapters ahead have been carefully planned after a review my observations, successes, research and hours of engagement in robust discussions with peers from various industries.

This book takes a holistic approach to the field of change management by considering the broader business environment in three key areas: Disruption, Industry Trends and Future of Work.

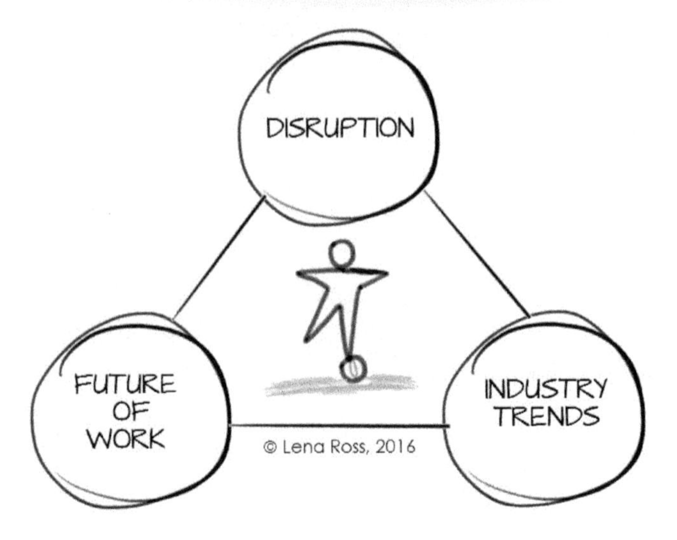

### *Disruption*

Digital disruption continues at a relentless pace. We now hear the word 'disruption' on a daily basis, and no industry is immune from it. It's not a fad. Unlike the end-to-end change management many of us have already led and managed, the current disruptive environment is continuous; there is no clear beginning, middle and end. With disruption comes challenge *and* opportunity. The opportunities can be found in new markets, improving the customer experience, leveraging the availability of knowledge and information through increased digital efficiencies and engaging through various social networks and platforms. There's an even greater opportunity to embrace it and develop new capabilities in everything we do.

The challenges cannot be met if the organisation and its leaders have a mindset that is reluctant to try new approaches.

Exploring emerging capabilities such as agile and learning mindsets, digital literacy, design thinking for human-centred solutions, and understanding hardwired human behaviour, will give us an edge in thinking like a start-up and taking faster, more relevant and iterative approaches to our practice. With these new capabilities, we are able to engage differently with our peers and customers, with greater empathy.

### *Industry trends*

In our fast-moving world, new discoveries are made, tested, applied and communicated very quickly. Information is so easily available. Through numerous social media channels, we can stay abreast of emerging trends and find out ways to apply them in our own business environment.

Recent findings are often consistent with what we already know and understand about human performance and leading through change, yet exploring new insights can challenge us to rethink the way in which we manage and lead our teams, and how we plan and deliver change.

For example, research in the field of neuroscience is providing us with fascinating insights into our hardwired human behaviour – how we think, our cognitive biases, how we decide, how we learn, how we respond to new situations and how we connect with others. The fields of cognitive and positive psychology, neuroscience, marketing and behavioural economics are helping us define new capabilities for leaders and change practitioners. The findings benefit us greatly, as with the use of neuro-imaging technology this field is undergoing unprecedented discovery. We can use these insights to take a closer look at how we interact with others and respond to change and new information, and how it affects human performance and productivity.

### *Future of work*

With disruption comes new industries and business models, resulting in many changes to the workplace and shifts in employee expectations and practices. This has led to an entire body of work around the 'future of work' or 'new ways of working' which explores the drivers behind the changing nature of work. Understanding the 'future of work' helps us prepare ourselves with 'future-ready' capabilities and thinking. Look at any online discussion or conference agenda on the future of work and you'll find a great deal of information around changes, not only in technology and digitisation. There are numerous insights on leadership styles, communication and engagement channels, social networks, diversity, globalisation, how we learn and network, our labour market, workplace flexibility, talent retention, generational expectations, innovation, and of course agility.

Technology is a blessing and a curse; the advent of robotics and Artificial Intelligence (AI) is likely to see some roles made defunct, while new ones emerge. Research carried out by the University of Oxford in 2016 reported that 57 percent of jobs across the OECD are at risk due to automation. For example, consider the app market, which didn't exist some ten years ago. It's now estimated to be a $77 billion industry, and growing.

And these are just a few elements ... keep on googling and you will keep on finding more!

The 'command and control' hierarchical leadership style is no longer resonating with employees. To keep up with the relentless changes, we need agile mindset mastery to embrace new skills and adapt quickly to changing circumstances. If we consider all these drivers with the impact of the Millennials in the workplace, we also see a different set of expectations, performance reward triggers and preferences about how work is carried out. It's predicted that Millennials will make up around 75% of our workforce by 2030.

## EXPERIMENTS AND HACKS

*Disruptive times call for disruptive and different approaches.* Some of my 'experiments' or 'hacks' that have worked may seem unconventional at first. All the ideas and tips can be applied regardless of the change framework you have in place. They can even be used if there is no structured methodology. To borrow a term that's often used in change management, it's *methodology-agnostic.* All the ideas have been tested in large-scale organisations, where most change is complex. If they have gained traction in an environment of large-scale change and complexity, they can be applied almost anywhere.

With all the nuances of business operations and people, only you can evaluate what will work best, or at least what is worth trying, at any point in time, in your organisation. If you are working in an environment with risk oversight and higher levels of governance and compliance, your change approach may take longer or need broader engagement.

If you use the model of *agile as a capability*, and consider hacks in each of the three layers - mindset, behaviours and practices - you will make progress in building agile as a capability in your organisation.

If you can't use the hacks straight away, use this book as a resource to look them up when you need them in future projects, or when the time is right. At the end of the book I've dedicated Chapter 18 to *Recapping the Hacks* so you can quickly find the hack you're looking for.

It's about hacking for change!

### *Finding your change hacks*

As the title of this book promises, you will find many hacks, with real examples, to help people embrace them, adopt them and play a role in co-creating the change. The proven ideas appear as ***#changehacks*** throughout the chapters. You will come across 52 numbered ***#changehacks*** starting from Chapter 4.

In recent years, the word *hack* has taken on a new meaning. Once associated with computer hacking, the term hack is now broadly used to describe *a shortcut, a solution or a useful tip to achieve something more efficiently.* In blogs now you will see tips with titles such as life hacks and customer hacks. On Twitter, you can follow experts of productivity hacks, beauty hacks and even hair hacks, among many others!

Consider a ***#changehack*** as one small thing you can do that has the potential to create a big impact, in terms of engagement, productivity, or mindset shift. It can be the one domino that has the capacity to knock over numerous dominoes, gaining momentum with each knock-down. Imagine instigating a few of these hacks and what can be achieved. To continue the domino metaphor, let's keep in mind that a single domino can bring down another domino that is 50 percent larger or heavier. How's that for g-force impact? Whether it's one hack at a time, or simultaneous hacks, you can make a great impact.

Each time you see a ***#changehack***, you'll find an explanation of what you can do.  Some of these hacks are also culture hacks. Some are a little disruptive and designed to challenge or nudge current mindsets. Most are designed to engage others to co-create change. And towards the end of the book, in Chapter 17, *So What, Now What?,* there's a couple for your personal and professional growth - your very own *#personalhacks*!

### Back matter

At the end of this book, there's a final chapter called *Back Matter*. In publishing parlance, this means the typical information that appears at the end of the main text: the bibliography and references.

The back matter in this book will prove useful for the immensely curious change hackers among you, as it contains:

- references, including relevant TED talks, clips and websites, and
- a glossary of commonly used terms from this book and other words related to agile projects.

### Who this book is for

This book is not just for people who would describe their occupation as dedicated change practitioners or consultants. Leading others through change is a responsibility that lies with a range of people in an organisation, from sponsors and senior leaders to programme and project managers. Leading change is now often identified as a key capability required of a leader.

The information and hacks in this book are for change consultants, leaders, project team members, change champions, human resources professionals, and generally for anyone interested in working in this area. The content is suitable for seasoned operators as well as people new to change management.

### What this book is not

Whilst this book will reference several theories, models and methodologies, there will be no great detail on them. There's a plethora of leadership and change management books that cover that content.

*As mentioned earlier in this chapter,* ***the focus is on the people side of change.***

Sadly, we can become so entrenched in systems, processes, frameworks and methodologies, that we forget the first principles of change: the *people* who are affected.

### *A jargon apology*

Love them or hate them, jargon, acronyms and abbreviations will not go away. So here is my apology in advance, as there will be a few acronyms coming your way, which will be explained. I've tried to keep them to a minimum, but better that you are familiar with the industry lingo than not.

Now...let's start hacking!

---

*'The difficulty lies not in new ideas, but from escaping old ones.'*
John Maynard Keynes

---

# 2 GETTING ON THE SAME PAGE WITH AGILE

While this book is about *hacking for agile change* on any type of project or change initiative, the focus is on a range of approaches that rely on agility. I have already defined agile as a capability made up three parts: mindset, behaviours and practice, all of which make up *organisational agility*.

In the workshops I run, I've learned that as a word, agile can mean different things to project and change people, or it can simply confuse them. Let's take a look at how agile is broadly defined, and how it will be applied in this book, in the context of hacking for change.

There are many entire books dedicated to agile as a project practice, being agile, doing agile and so on. This chapter is designed to provide an introduction, and to explain the difference between the software development context and the broader application of the word agile.

## BIG A, LITTLE A

Here's a likely scenario. You are chatting to a colleague and the 'a-' word crops up in conversation. Then your agile-savvy colleague asks: *Oh, do you mean agile with a big A or agile with a little a?*

Let's look at what this means, and how you can clarify the definitions and get on the same page as your stakeholders when you need to. I've discovered that the two versions of the word 'agile' - capitalised and all lower case - are often used interchangeably.

To start the conversation, I draw the following diagram on a sheet of paper in my notebook. I deliberately draw it in front of them, as opposed to providing a printed version, to invite input.

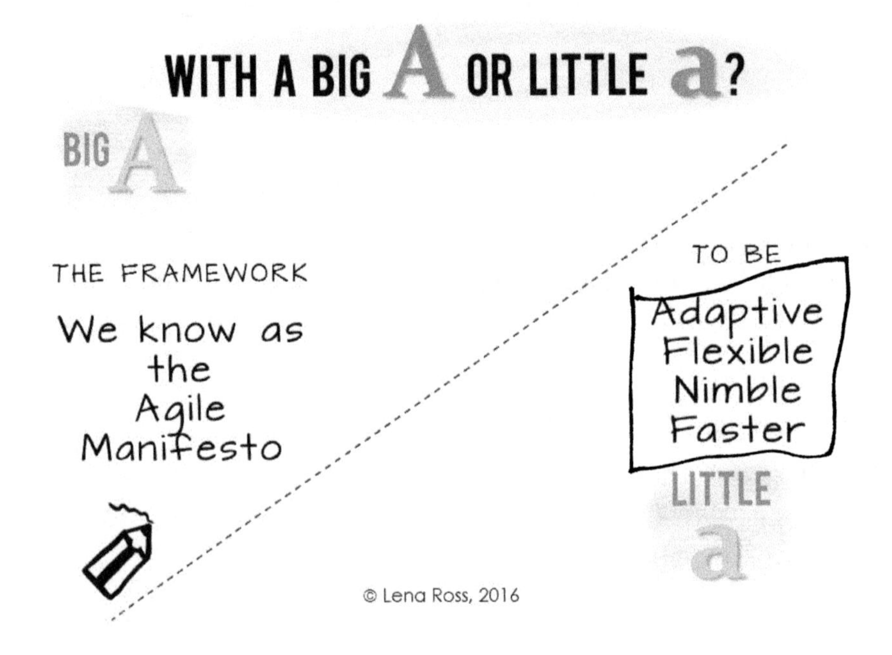


In my workshops, I prepare the same diagram on flipchart paper. There is white space to invite participants to add their thoughts and definitions throughout the session.

I explain that it's common practice in the Agile community to use the *big A* when referring to the Agile Manifesto and its associated practices. The *little a* is the adjective we use to describe something that is adaptive, flexible, nimble, quicker of mind and faster in movement. An athlete is nimble in action just as an insightful thinker is agile of mind.

You can start the conversation in the same way to get your team on the same page with what 'agile' means. Perhaps we need to be agile about how we define agile?

*I've used this description to help illustrate the difference:*

When an organisation wants to become more agile, they look for ways to be responsive to external forces, be adaptive, deliver services and products to customers faster, think outside the box, and eliminate waste to improve effectiveness. To *help them* achieve this, they have recruited coaches and project managers who have experience in Agile software and product development. These projects using Agile practices alone will not make the organisation agile, as that also requires people with the right mindset and behaviours. Agile (yes, big A) project approaches will help, but will not achieve this alone.

In this book, the hacks and tips are largely focused on the *little a* agile - what the word meant, and still does, before the Agile Manifesto was invented. To reiterate a message from the previous chapter, you will uncover ideas and examples that you can use on both *big A* activities and *little a* activities. The goal here is not to hold off 'change hacking' just because you are not working on an official Agile project.

### *The history of BIG A*

To provide some clarity on Agile (with a *big A*), let's take a brief look at where it started. If you've been reading or talking about Agile/agile, no doubt you've heard of the ***Agile Manifesto.***

The Agile Manifesto, designed for software development, was written back in 2001. Its intent was not to be anti-methodology; rather, it was to bring about a balanced view that would welcome adjustments and pace. In the manifesto we can see the elements that are core to change practitioners in an agile world: a focus on the customer, a nimble approach and value placed on people over process.

The Agile Manifesto is made up of:

- Four values
- 12 principles.

### *Agile values*

The values mantra states that:

---

*While there is value in the items on the right, we value the items on the left more.*

---

**THE AGILE MANIFESTO**
A STATEMENT OF VALUES

OVER

| | |
|---|---|
| Individuals & interactions | Processes & tools |
| Working software | Comprehensive documentation |
| Customer collaboration | Contract negotiation |
| Responding to change | Following a plan |

**SOURCE:** www.agilemanifesto.org

*Agile principles*

The Agile Manifesto's 12 principles:

- Our highest priority is to satisfy the customer through early and continuous delivery of valuable software.
- Welcome changing requirements, even late in development. Agile processes harness change for the customer's competitive advantage.
- Deliver working software frequently, from a couple of weeks to a couple of months, with a preference to the shorter timescale.
- Business people and developers must work together daily throughout the project.
- Build projects around motivated individuals. Give them the environment and support they need, and trust them to get the job done.
- The most efficient and effective method of conveying information to and within a development team is face-to-face conversation.
- Working software is the primary measure of progress.
- Agile processes promote sustainable development. The sponsors, developers, and users should be able to maintain a constant pace indefinitely.
- Continuous attention to technical excellence and good design enhances agility.
- Simplicity--the art of maximizing the amount of work not done--is essential.
- The best architectures, requirements, and designs emerge from self-organizing teams.
- At regular intervals, the team reflects on how to become more effective, then tunes and adjusts its behaviour accordingly.

Source: www.agilemanifesto.org

While the values and principles are software-centric, the application can be extended to non-software projects, especially with the themes of lean, team behaviours and customer-centricity.

We can see how the principles and value of *big A* also apply to *little a*. But *little a* is agile about everything, with an application that is broader, particularly in reference to an organisation being agile.

### *Busting myths about Agile*

The definitions of *big A* and *little a* can cause confusion. This makes it easy for Agile/agile sceptics to jump to conclusions that have given Agile/agile some bad press. You'll hear or read about myths, most of which are not true. Some make Agile/agile sound like complete anarchy.

Here are some common myths to explode right now:

#### *Myth 1: Agile is just scrum*

*Reality*: Scrum is a framework for developing and managing work. Agile is an umbrella word for practices such as Scrum, so Scrum is one of many practices belonging to Agile. Agile is so much more!

#### *Myth 2: Agile means no plan*

*Reality:* Planning is different, not absent. Up-front planning is replaced with a more iterative, adaptive process. This means you will see numerous revised plans, not just one plan. There are more plans developed at a greater frequency due to the iterative nature of regular review. The Agile Manifesto's 12 principles ensure that Agile is not anarchy.

#### *Myth 3: Agile means no project managers*

*Reality:* Agile management definitely needs project managers. They are often called Scrum Masters. Team roles are different, demanding a different type of leadership and team dynamic, and ultimately this is how work gets done.

### *Myth 4: Agile means no documentation*

*Reality:* This may be wishful thinking for some, but documentation has a place in Agile. There are design documents that add value by providing information on the Minimum Viable Product (MVP). Documentation is iterative with records of all previous versions and documents that drive (not replace) conversations with stakeholders. MVP refers to an artefact with enough features or information to demonstrate or provide a solution.

### *Myth 5: Agile only works for developers*

*Reality:* Whilst Agile started with a focus on software development, it's now been applied more broadly. Any project type can use Agile approaches to improve delivery.

### *Myth 6: Agile is the silver bullet*

*Reality:* Really? Find me a silver bullet and we will all be out of jobs! Agile is not the panacea for all our organisational challenges. It needs the right leadership, behaviours and mindset to support it. Agile practices alone will not make your business nimble and adaptive.

## SO WHAT IS AGILE CHANGE MANAGEMENT?

This question has been circulating in the change industry for some time. I would define agile change management as a *practice that draws on the ethos of the Agile Manifesto, to adaptively deliver the right solution at the right time.*

Let's take a closer look at this.

### ***Adaptively deliver***

To be adaptive in your delivery means you can respond to changing requirements and adjust your change plans. I've seen many change managers express disappointment or frustration over the need to recast their plans to adjust to shifting goals.

Adaptive delivery requires a nimble, or agile, mindset. In Part One on *How We Think,* we will look at embracing ambiguity and developing a more adaptive mindset.

Let go of the need for perfection, especially if you are attached to the need to develop a perfect document before you circulate it. I have a passion for infographics and material with high visual impact. It took me a (long) while to learn that I was spending a wee bit too much time perfecting my visuals. I learned that having a stakeholder meeting with an 'imperfect' artefact is okay: manage expectations and explain that your document is in draft and that you are covering points for *discussion and iteration.* Drawing on a whiteboard or flip chart paper was a way of discussing the change that promoted a good deal more co-creation and engagement than rocking up to a meeting with a big, colourful PowerPoint slide deck. The very fact that a document doesn't have a high gloss finish invites collaboration. When I saw the value of taking this approach, it shifted my thinking to 'adaptive delivery'.

This is also consistent with the Agile Manifesto value of *individuals and interactions over processes and tools*, and the principle of *simplicity*, which means to right-size our work.

### The right solution

One of my MBA university lecturers, on the topic of project management, often told us: *Don't use a sledgehammer to crack an egg!*

It's a thought that's stayed with me. I've used his quote many times to remind myself, and others, that the right solution starts with right-sizing our plan and approach.

This is where the Agile principles spill over into what we do every day.

Take the software out of the equation, and we still need to consider what is right for the customer, how we can do it most efficiently and be adaptive in the way we plan and deliver change in an agile way.

For a long time, where linear, waterfall-style projects were mainstream, change was often delivered in a linear approach with a list of artefacts to complete. Now, in a climate of complex and continuous change, there is an increasing expectation that change programmes will be leaner and deliver outcomes in shorter cycles.

The pressure is on the change practitioner to be increasingly adaptive in their approach. What worked on a project in the bank three years ago is unlikely to hit the mark as an approach on a project today in health care. In one of my blog posts, I refer to right-sizing the change effort as *Goldilocks change management*. In the familiar fairy tale of the three bears, we read about Goldilocks' three options: one that is too much, one that is too little and one that is just right. In this parable, there's a case for applying the Goldilocks principle in how we deliver change.

The Swedes have a word that captures this beautifully – *lagom*. The word translates to mean *not too little, not too much, just right. Lagom* is about being lean and clever in your approach so you deliver what is 'just right'.

The term *Minimum Viable Product* (MVP), mentioned earlier, is fast becoming commonly used in project and change parlance. It means delivering a product or artefact with just enough features or information to achieve your objectives or kick off your conversation. But MVP doesn't mean we totally discard our change management toolkit. It means the change practitioner needs to be adaptive and ***aware of*** when to scale up or down.

The nature of right-sizing in itself means there's no prescription on how to be like Goldilocks. The scope and scale of the change initiative helps you size your work. The variables are countless and the possibilities are numerous. Experience and confidence help, of course, as does an agile mindset.

### *The right time*

In the spirit of the Goldilocks metaphor, scheduling change management activity in the right doses, at the right time, is critical. Engage your users too late and they will feel disconnected. Involve them too early, and there may not be enough information available to articulate the reason for the change. Involve people as soon as they can play a meaningful role in the co-creation of the change.

Again, there are no prescribed guidelines on when the right time will arrive. It relies on staying connected with your project team and your key stakeholders. Look for clues such as when impacted users start asking questions or showing interest in the changes ahead. The right time to kick off your engagement and communications is ideally before rumours trigger a negative message about your change initiative.

Taking a Goldilocks approach to delivering change helps us consider what is fit for purpose, to provide valuable change support for our stakeholders and end users. The change hacks in this book will help you *right-size* your change plan and schedule interventions at the *optimal time*.

All these parts make up Agile, agile, and agile change management. If we consider these two things:

- the Agile Manifesto is a representation of *big A Agile*
- agile, adaptive practices and thinking represent *little a agile,*

then what is the role of the project leader, the change leader and change practitioner in this agile world? The next three parts will unpack this for you.

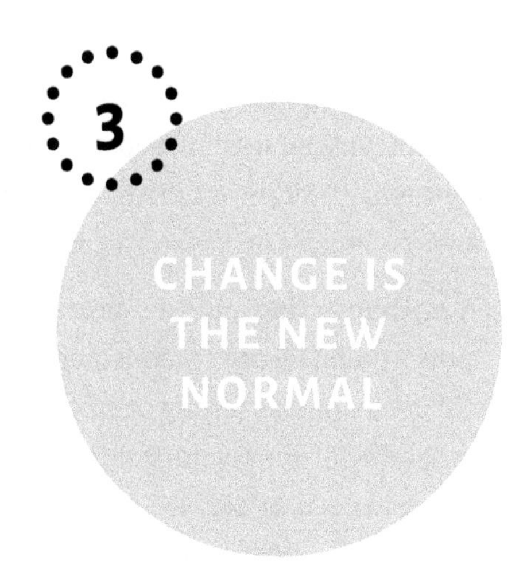


Before launching into agile mindset, behaviours and practice, I've put one chapter aside to reflect on the disruptive environment in which we work, live, and to which we continually adapt.

Can you imagine your day without your smart phone? As recently as 10 years ago there were no iPhones. You were probably listening to music on your iPod, or perhaps even CDs. You took photos with a digital camera – yes, a separate device! And you jumped on your desktop computer to surf the net and send and receive emails. Your social media, if you were an early-ish adopter, was probably a profile on Myspace.

Do you remember resisting any of these changes to your personal and professional life? Now look at you! Bets are on you've been digitally disrupted!

## THE SANDS ARE SHIFTING

And what about the world around us? The industries we've worked in, products and services we use? If you consider what else has happened in the last 10 years, you'll see that disruption is relentless. The world's largest taxi company, Uber, owns no vehicles; the largest accommodation provider, AirBNB, owns no properties; the fastest growing banks, such as SocietyOne, have no actual money; and the world's largest movie house,

Netflix, owns no cinemas. And the list goes on. We can see that digital disruption has well and truly arrived with no signs of easing. To mention one more, take a moment to consider what driver-less cars will do to the way we move around and the impact on associated industries.

This accelerated speed of change demands an unprecedented agility to remain competitive. Conventional business models are vulnerable. Chaos has replaced certainty. The businesses failing to survive are the ones not seeing the signals, not adapting or simply not keeping up with the pace of change. Because something worked in the past does not guarantee repeat success. Business leaders can no longer look to the past for clues on how to manage the future, let alone the present.

### *The VUCA world*

It's no surprise that in this environment of digital disruption, we are hearing more about the need for *adaptive leadership*. Businesses must become more proactively *adaptive*, or *agile,* to try things and learn from failure fast, deliver solutions to the customer more quickly and take a truly human-centred design approach to product, service and nimble delivery.

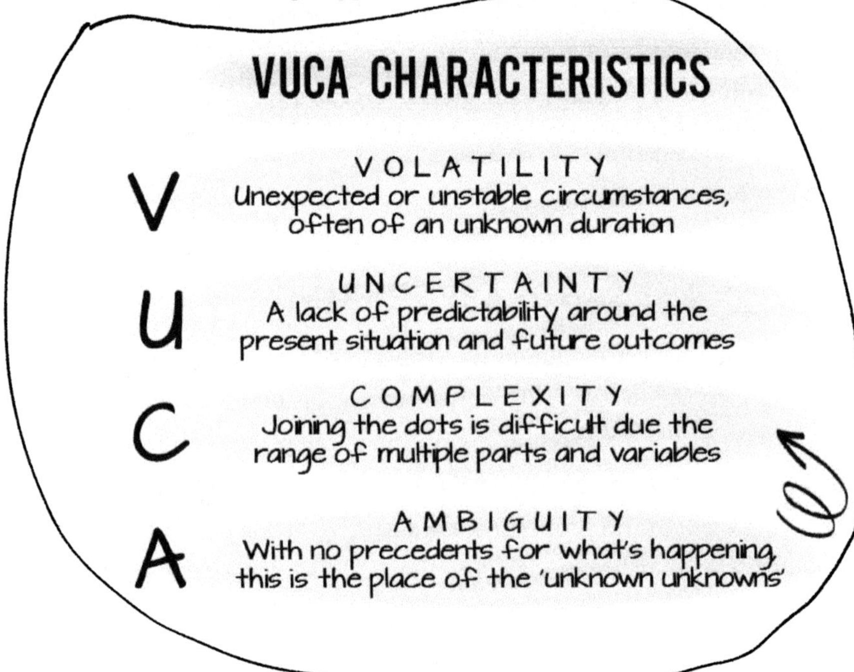

This environment is now often referred to as VUCA (pronounced voo-ka). This acronym for *volatility, uncertainty, complexity* and *ambiguity* was coined by the US military back in the late 1990s, but has really gained momentum in the last decade. Now, it's increasingly relevant in a business context, as decision making is becoming increasingly complex.

### *The disruptors become the disrupted*

We also know things are moving so fast that today's disruptor can easily be tomorrow's disrupted. By way of example, let's take the last 30 years in the music industry. We saw the record player that played vinyls replaced by the CD player and Walkman (in between somewhere there were cassette tapes), to be replaced by MP3 players and iTunes. More recently, Spotify has entered the market, providing music on demand without the need to download files. This is one of numerous examples across many industries.

So how do leaders stay up-to-date in a rapidly changing world? The conventional model of attending leadership programmes and learning on the job or through coaching may not keep up with the calibre of skills needed to succeed in a VUCA environment.

We need to continually build on our existing skills, refreshing our capability profile with the emerging capabilities required in a VUCA world.

### *Navigating VUCA*

***VUCA presents a paradox.*** Whilst we cannot predict the future based on the past, we need to make sense of it, accelerate our delivery, accept our failures as a learning experience and be sufficiently nimble to quickly adjust and improve through numerous short-cycle iterations.

Instead of shying away from a complex environment that's here to stay, we need to explore approaches that support our businesses and offer us insights into what we can do when we deliver change.

### *Change is no longer a process*

As change influencers and leaders, we have new challenges to navigate this VUCA world where change is the new normal. Up until now, much of our methodology, frameworks and practice, has been based on theoretical change models that define change as a linear process, with a clear beginning and end. For example, Kurt Lewin's model explains organisational change as a process of unfreezing, changing and refreezing. So what happens now, when our organisations are in a constant state of the 'middle bit' with little or no time to refreeze? A defined end state has less relevance in an environment that's continuously disrupted.

Many organisations have already understood the benefits of adopting agile as a framework for building self-organising, multi-disciplinary teams. The Netherlands-based bank ING adopted this approach in 2015 and has reported productivity gains and speed to market. It's important to note that in industries like banks, which need to manage risk and monitor compliance, the introduction of agile practices needs to be scaled to accommodate these industry nuances.

Once seen as the domain of start-up companies such as Spotify, the agile ways of working are the new ways of working. Large businesses with a hierarchical organisational architecture are exploring the what, the why and most importantly the how, for adopting these agile principles to shift their culture and remain relevant in a competitive market.

The VUCA environment demands from leaders, and particularly from change practitioners, a refresh of our capabilities to stay current and to rethink our approach to advising on and supporting change. So what does change mastery look like in a VUCA world?

## WHEN CHANGE IS A 'PROJECT'

In many organisations, change is delivered as an end-to-end project, using what is often referred to as a traditional 'waterfall' approach. The terms 'waterfall' and 'Agile', as project methodologies, typically apply to software development and technology-based implementations. To make the distinction, here are brief definitions:

### *Waterfall*

A conventional waterfall approach, often referred to as a Software Development Life Cycle (SDLC), comprises discrete project phases such as plan, analyse, design, develop, test and implement. This is a linear, sequential model that assumes one phase is complete before moving to the next one. In this approach, there's an emphasis on documenting processes, design and requirements, signing them off as final and developing the solution.

### *Agile*

The Agile approach favours an incremental, iterative approach with shorter cycles over the linear approach used in waterfall. Each 'iteration' produces a working product to present to end users and stakeholders to gain feedback that is incorporated in the next or future iterations. Agile is not just about being fast because we know first to market is not always the most successful or enduring one in the market. Some of you will remember that MySpace pre-dated Facebook and there were search engines with the names of Excite, Alta Vista, Ask Jeeves, HotBot and Yahoo (to name just a few) around, before the one we now also use as a verb – Google.

## AGILE AND LEAN

The term 'agile' is often interchanged with the word 'lean'. Lean means efficient and reducing waste, in a Kaizen or continuous improvement context.

Agile, as a term and approach (*little a* and *Big A*), is more aligned with our VUCA environment and disruption. Agile projects can better accommodate changes to requirements, deliver faster in shorter iterations and feedback loops. As we've seen in the Agile Manifesto, Agile demonstrates a stronger focus on face-to-face involvement throughout each iteration, making it more human-centred with a continuous focus on value and continuous improvement.

We know that change isn't always delivered as an end-to-end technology implementation. In disruption, we need constant change and review in the areas of product development, service delivery, organisational structures, business operating models, mindsets, behaviours and culture. When ***change is the new normal***, it's the practices and behaviours from Agile project teams that are useful to explore and apply.

## CHANGE MASTERY

There's an urban myth that change management is simply about delivering communications and training. This is a clear indicator that change management is misunderstood in many circles. This myth may have stemmed from a couple of sources:

- early change management practice, before specific capabilities were defined
- the smaller-scale business-as-usual process of change, where communications and training support can effectively implement the change,

and possibly from various other sources. Like all urban myths, this one is fictional and of obscure origin, so it's time to explode yet another myth with the reality!

### *At an enterprise level*

If we apply a holistic view in an organisation, enterprise change mastery needs strong change capability in ***three key groups of professionals*** who are responsible for ensuring that the new ways are adopted and embedded:

1 | Change leaders – this group is made up of project sponsors, program/project managers and senior leaders who are either decision makers or recommenders;

2 | Program and project directors - who are responsible for the *implementation* of the change initiative;

3 | Change practitioners – these are the dedicated change professionals, who are either employed in a dedicated change role or contracted in for their specialist skills to advise on and support the change delivery to ensure *adoption* of the change.

### *Change leaders and sponsors*

The *change leaders* and *sponsors* will find, if they are working in larger organisations, that the capability of 'leading through change' is likely to appear in their leadership capability framework.

Sponsors and senior leaders have the 'formal' authority, based on their positional power, to endorse the transformation. They need to be highly visible and seen to be actively committed to the cause. To 'lead' change across an organisation is to role-model the new, desired behaviours and mindset, and influence stakeholders to embrace and sustain the evolving circumstances in the business.

The skills that support strong change leadership are a learning, adaptive mindset, comfort with ambiguity, visibility, communicating with influence, customer-centric focus, personal resilience and digital literacy.

### *Program and project directors*

The *program/project directors* implement the change by taking a structured approach to identifying the scope, tasks and activities to achieve the project's objectives. This involves managing budgets, risks and issues along with team management and reporting back to the sponsor and senior stakeholders.

### *Change practitioners*

The dedicated *change practitioner* is the specialist who advises, influences or is consulted on introducing and embedding the change. Their role is to ensure that the impacted people are ready to *adopt* the new ways. To do this, there is a set of functional and behavioural capabilities that form part of this specialist's toolkit.

A change practitioner should aim to have a broad set of capabilities made up of three parts:

**1** | Core functional capabilities that specifically relate to their dedicated role;

**2** | Behavioural and general (non-change-specific) capabilities that complement their role, and are expected of change leaders and program/project directors;

**3** | Emerging capabilities.

Each capability type provides the change practitioner with a different form of skill fitness, outlined in the following table. The core, functional capabilities enable you to plan and support change delivery, typically in a more conventional end-to-end waterfall project. These are the skills we need for *'match fitness'* for our day-to-day activity. The more generic capabilities are needed for *'business fitness'* and they serve us well in any role in an organisation. We must always consider our *'evolutionary fitness'* by looking out for emerging trends and the capabilities we need in a disruptive environment, and to future-proof our career.

***Holistic capability overview for change mastery***

| Capability type | Fitness Genre | Examples |
|---|---|---|
| Core, functional | Match Fitness | • Change planning and delivery<br>• Change impact assessments<br>• Business engagement and stakeholder management<br>• Learning / training - needs analysis, design, delivery and/or evaluation<br>• Communication<br>• Assessing change readiness<br>• Organisation design<br>• Understanding of project management |
| Behavioural & general | Business Fitness | • Emotional intelligence<br>• Strategic thinking<br>• Analysis and problem solving<br>• Facilitation<br>• Networking and connecting<br>• Business acumen |
| Emerging | Evolutionary Fitness | • Understanding the future of work<br>• Design thinking<br>• Agile mindset<br>• Digital literacy<br>• Understanding hardwired human behaviour/neuroscience |

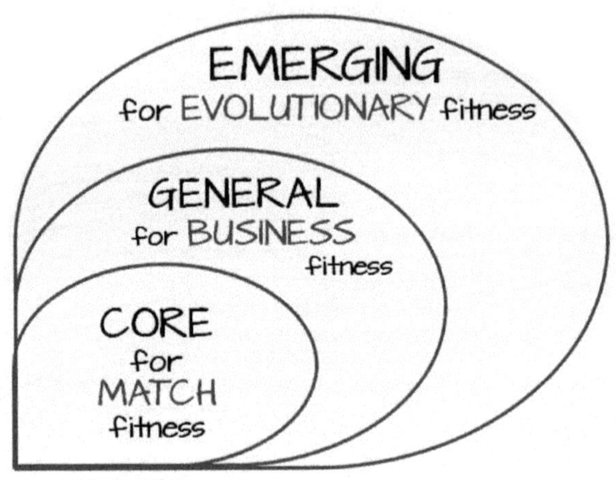


### *Core change capabilities for match fitness*

A dedicated change practitioner is expected to have a set of ***core capabilities*** to carry out their role. These are the functional skills that directly relate to a change management role. Recruiters or interviewers will ask questions to assess proven experience, and in some cases, examples of artefacts to demonstrate how you apply these skills.

Project resourcing decisions are often determined by the core capabilities of the change practitioner, as project types may require different skills. For example, a major organisational restructure may call for specialist skills in stakeholder engagement and organisational design. A technology implementation may need specific skills in learning and instructional design.

You need to practise these to become better at what you do, and you will achieve this by immersing yourself in it, watching others and coaching others in these core skills. This skill set keeps us 'fit' and ready for our day-to-day activity, so we need these for 'match fitness'.

*General and behavioural capabilities for business fitness*

This list is not exhaustive and the capabilities are not unique to change folk, but they are skills we need to complement our core capability toolkit. They provide us with a 'commercial' or 'business fitness', as they are valuable skills that we can take to any role.

*Emerging change capabilities for evolutionary fitness*

Emerging capabilities are the ones we need to develop to remain current in this disruptive environment and to demonstrate a future-forward focus. This type of fitness needs conscious effort with an agile mindset to support self-managed learning and the adoption of new practices.

These capabilities are dynamic and ever-changing. By being adaptive and embracing new information and approaches, we demonstrate 'evolutionary fitness' in our industry.

We need to keep an eye on developing and maintaining all three types of capabilities for a holistic change management approach and to stay ahead of the curve!

## ORGANISATIONAL AGILITY

The online business dictionary describes organisational agility as:

> *'The capability of a company to rapidly change or adapt in response to changes in the market. A high degree of organizational agility can help a company to react successfully to the emergence of new competitors, the development of new industry-changing technologies, or sudden shifts in overall market conditions.'*

An agile organisation can respond quickly and identify opportunities ahead of their competitors, so they can deliver what the customer wants more quickly. Agility is the competitive advantage needed, particularly in the current turbulent landscape, to drive revenue and business sustainability.

### *What makes an organisation agile?*

You will recall that the model I developed to define *agile as a capability* features 'organisational agility' as the supporting tier at the base. This representation shows that for an organisation to become agile, it needs people who demonstrate the agile mindset and behaviours and can apply the practices.

This will rely on recruiting the right people, clearly defining the capabilities needed, and rewarding existing employees for demonstrating the desired mindset, behaviours and practices.

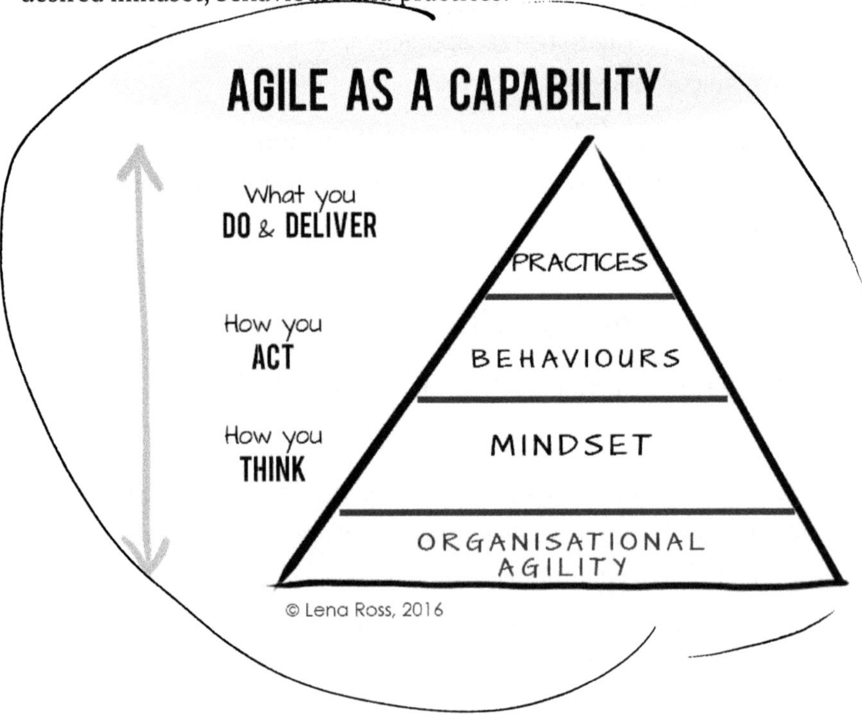


### *From knowing to doing*

Knowing about these capabilities, or attending a course to find out about them, is one thing. How do we know if a change practitioner has mastered these capabilities, and more importantly, has a track record in their application? Of course, a good recruiter or interviewer will uncover the depth of experience with expert questioning.

How do we take it from *knowing to doing?* Knowledge does not necessarily translate to execution. But good examples, or hacks, on how to experiment with different low-risk or no-risk approaches is a good start. And that's where we start the journey with *change hacks.* Onwards and upwards!

# HOW YOU THINK

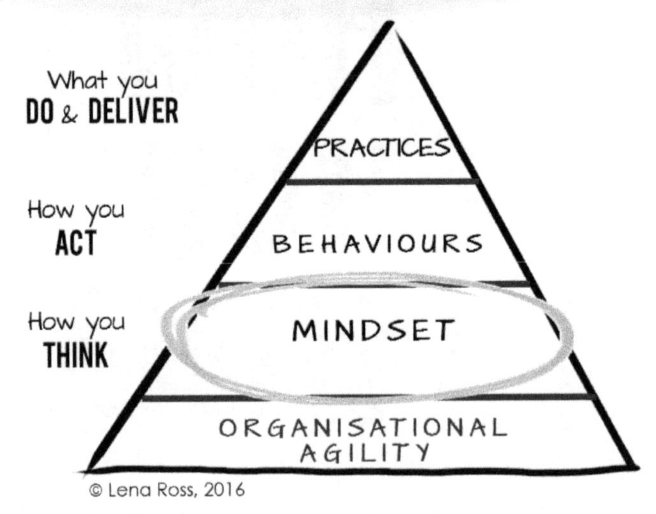
AGILE AS A CAPABILITY
What you
DO & DELIVER
How you
ACT
How you
THINK
PRACTICES
BEHAVIOURS
MINDSET
ORGANISATIONAL
AGILITY
© Lena Ross, 2016

## MAKING SENSE OF AGILITY

In the VUCA environment, change practitioners will typically find themselves landing in more projects that follow agile practices. Change frameworks and approaches are quickly adjusting to align to this way of delivery. With agile change practices fast becoming part of the change toolkit, we *also* need to adopt agility in our behaviours and thinking.

*Agility is not just about a skillset or a methodology, it's also a mindset. So, what does agility in practice look like? How do we make sense of agility? And more importantly, how do we achieve it? It starts with the mindset.*

## HOW YOU THINK

Our mindset is our set of attitudes and beliefs. In other words, our mindset is about *how we think.* We often don't stop to actually think about how we think, or how others around us think. Yet our mindset underpins our behaviours, our choices and how we apply our capabilities. It can be a blessing or a curse; it can either make or break our professional and personal potential. Let's find out why, and what we can do about it.

### *It starts with the mindset*

Agility in mindset is a combination of various approaches and thinking. It's versatile, adaptive and nimble in decision making. It demonstrates a tolerance for ambiguity, with a resilience to changing goal posts and uncertainty. It's a curious mind hungry for new information, with the qualities of what is defined as a 'learning mindset'.

We need to be open to new ideas and ways of working, so we are nimble enough to change tack when the winds take a different direction.

## THE ANATOMY OF THE 'AGILE' MINDSET

There are numerous definitions on what it means to be agile, take an agile approach to projects and change, and to have an agile mindset. Based on the practices that are becoming more widespread in organisations, along with external forces demanding shorter, more adaptive delivery cycles, here are four characteristics that make up the anatomy of the mindset of an agile individual:

**1** | Open to new ideas - a growth and learning mindset;

**2** | Adopting a beginner's mindset - building resilience and curiosity;

**3** | Embracing ambiguity and uncertainty - an ability to work within the unknown, without answers;

**4** | Design thinking - taking a human-centred approach to engagement and developing solutions, with empathy for the end user and customer.

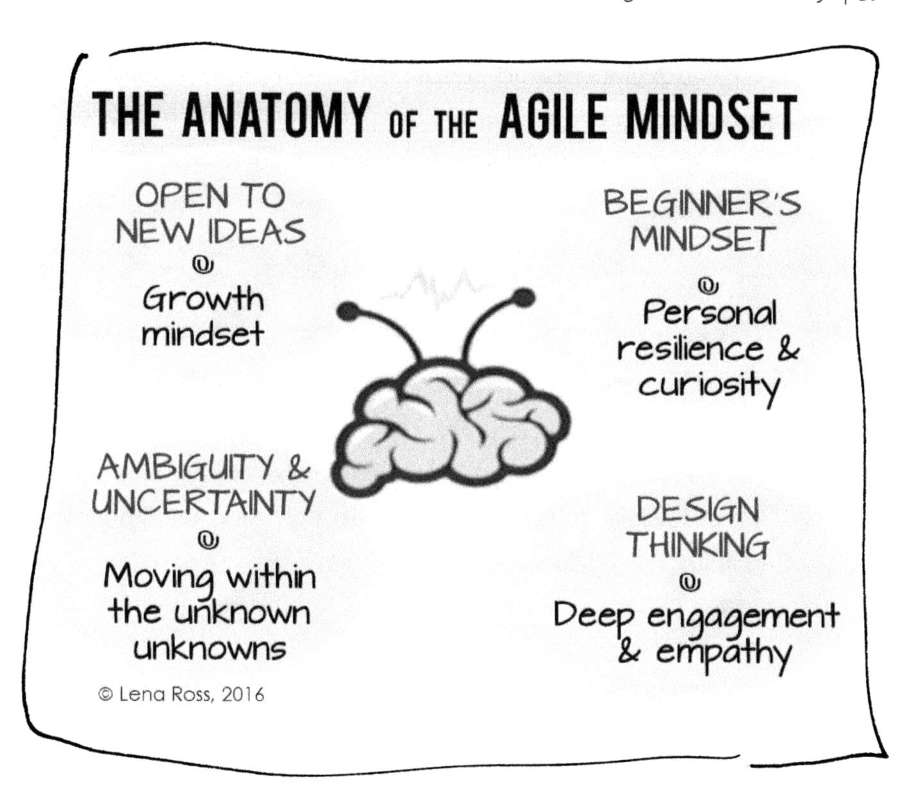


***How do you rate?***

Let's start with a quick, informal self-assessment.

Use the following statements to rate your level of comfort:

*Open to new ideas - growth mindset*

- I can learn from constructive feedback.
- I am inspired by others' success.
- I believe that if you practise something for long enough, you can develop a talent for it.
- I'm happy to choose a challenge over an easier option.

*Thinking like a beginner*

- I can anticipate future consequences and issues.
- I'm comfortable with other disruptive practices such as openly sharing my work in progress, even when it's not complete.
- I consider failures and mistakes as opportunities to learn and improve.

- I like to explore new ground, demonstrating curiosity and asking questions.
- I will question things I already understand to uncover how other users perceive the world.
- I look for themes and patterns to connect various interactions with people.
- I listen wholeheartedly without thinking about what I want to say next.

*Embracing ambiguity and uncertainty*

- I am comfortable asking questions to make sense of ambiguity.
- I can take an iterative approach to my work, realigning and readjusting quickly.
- I can take action without having the full picture (all the requirements).
- I can move on to the next piece of work without fully completing a previous piece of work.
- I can manage stakeholder expectations around uncertainty and iterative approaches.
- I am comfortable facilitating without PowerPoint slides.
- I am comfortable facilitating without answers.
- I am adaptable when direction or priorities change.

*Design Thinking*

- I am comfortable walking through visual boards with stakeholders and my project team.
- I am able to link variables to devise possible scenarios.
- I take a macro view of the business environment when developing solutions.
- I am open to observing body language and asking questions to gain deep understanding of my end users.
- In a brainstorming session, I park judgement and accept all ideas as possibilities.

How did you rate? This isn't a magazine-style quiz where you add up your score and read about your agility profile. It's designed to be a simple checklist to help you become aware of the characteristics that comprise an agile mindset.

## THE GROWTH MINDSET

A growth mindset, often referred to as a learning mindset as opposed to a fixed one, thrives on challenge and welcomes failure as an opportunity to learn and improve. According to Carol Dweck, author of the book, *Mindset, A new psychology of success,* someone with a growth mindset is prepared to step outside their comfort zone, take a risk and be willing to stretch themselves. People with a fixed mindset believe that talent and intelligence is just that - fixed. With the notion that capability is static, a fixed-mindset individual will not venture outside their comfort zone due to a fear of failure.

If you have a fixed mindset, you will be concerned with how you will be judged. Contrast this with the person with the growth mindset who has a focus on self-improvement.

### *Quick guide to the indicators*

The following diagram shows characteristics for the fixed mindset and growth mindset.

## FIXED vs GROWTH MINDSET

| INTELLIGENCE IS STATIC | INTELLIGENCE CAN BE DEVELOPED |
|---|---|
| Avoids challenges | Embraces challenges |
| Gives up easily | Persists in obstacles |
| Sees efforts as failures | Sees efforts as necessary |
| Ignores useful feedback | Learns from feedback |
| Threatened by others' success | Inspired by others' success |

**SOURCE**: Dweck, C. (2006) *Mindset: A new psychology of success*

### *From fixed to growth*

You are probably wondering if it's possible to develop a growth mindset. The answer is yes. Awareness is the first step. Understanding what comprises a fixed or growth mindset helps you identify fixed vs growth mindset characteristics in yourself and in others. In Chapter 6, *Mindset Hacks,* you'll find techniques to further develop your level of awareness to shift your mindset.

This takes us to our first *#changehack*!

### *#changehack 1 - listen to your self-talk*

See if you can *catch yourself out!*

Here are some typical phrases, either said aloud or as inner self-talk, that represent the fixed and growth mindsets:

| Fixed mindset | Growth mindset |
|---|---|
| • We've tried that before and it failed. | • Even though we've tried that before, we'll find out why it didn't work and have another crack at it. |
| • That's not in my job description. | • I don't usually do that; however, the experience and exposure will be good for me. |
| • I can't do that - I've never been good at <insert your activity>. | • I've never done that before, but I'd like to give it a go. |
| • I didn't get good grades at school so I'm not good at learning new things. | • School may not have been the best learning environment for me; there are so many other ways to learn new things and grow. |
| • That won't work around here. | • Let's explore some approaches that will work with our people here. |
| • No one will buy that/agree to that. | • Let's hack through the systems and processes here to make it work. |
| • I can't crunch the numbers, I've never been good at maths. | • I'll have a go at crunching the numbers, may need some help though. |
| • I am going to look so silly if I try that and fail. | • There is always something new to learn. |
| • We need to get this right the first time. | • If we don't get it right the first time, we'll learn and try again. |
| • There are too many problems to overcome. | • This problem is an opportunity to come up with a workaround/hack. |
| • I don't like to make mistakes. | • When I make a mistake, I look for the lesson. |

In her book, Dweck explains a mindset shift with the example of the movie *Groundhog Day*. The film plot features the protagonist Phil Connors, played by Bill Murray, who starts out with a fixed mindset. As each day repeats itself over, Phil continues to apply his arrogance for self-gratification. But as each day goes by, frustration mounts. He slowly begins to realise that to break this monotonous time-warp, he needs to shift his thinking. Aha! This breakthrough moment occurs through iterative learning, where Connors makes one small change at a time in his decisions. By using this extra 'groundhog' time for learning and helping others, he's finally released from the spell.

Okay, so we won't have *Groundhog Day* moments to help us reach a mindset epiphany. But we can be aware of what a fixed vs growth mindset looks like, and catch ourselves out when our self-talk is sounding like Phil Connors.

*If you keep doing the same thing the same way, you will get the same results!*

There are no mistakes, only lessons.

## EMBRACING AMBIGUITY

Embracing ambiguity means to be comfortable with uncertainty and the unknown. It's a leap of faith in thinking. When we are uncomfortable with ambiguity, it's easy to jump to conclusions and make assumptions to anchor our thinking to something familiar and safe. This is the anchor that limits us from exploring new ideas.

Once we embrace uncertainty, our minds are open to new possibilities, which in turn can evolve into 'aha' moments or breakthrough solutions.

*"We may not know what that answer is, but we know that we have to give ourselves permission to explore."*
Patrice Martin, Creative Director and Co-Lead, IDEO.org

The next chapter will explain how Design Thinking starts from a place of not knowing, making ambiguity a prerequisite for exploring before reaching a solution.

In her book *The Power of Pause,* Nance Guilmartin talks about the value of pausing, reflecting and exploring all options before reaching decisions, as we often default to rushing in the busy-ness of our lives. She acknowledges that we operate in a climate of uncertainty and relentless change, which adds to the complexity of making decisions and taking action.

There's a powerful message in this quote from her book:

*"I'm not here to make you comfortable with change.*
*I'm here to help you be comfortable with your discomfort."*
Nance Guilmartin

Change is taking place and will continue to do so. Change is not an option. We can help others through the discomfort it may cause, but we can't make change go away.

### #changehack 2 - think like a beginner

To think like a start-up is to accept a healthy dose of risk and learn quickly from failure along the way.

If we can think like a start-up, or assume a beginner's mindset, we can focus on suspending judgement. Too many times, we've heard people say, *Oh we've already tried that, it doesn't work.* The fact is if you try again with only a small variable, such as timing, it could work. You are probably familiar with the many stories and quotes about Thomas Edison. We often hear that the inventor made around 1,000 attempts before inventing the light bulb. One report even states that when he was asked how it felt to fail 1,000 times, Edison replied, "*I didn't fail 1,000 times. The light bulb was an invention with 1,000 steps.*" How's that for a learning mindset?

Change can't happen if you are deterred by the fear of failure. Reframe your view of failure to one of experiment.

To have a beginner's mindset is to be intensely curious.

- Find patterns
- Suspend judgement
- Listen properly
- Question everything.

## THE CASE FOR CURIOSITY

What have you learned, by intent or chance, from being curious? After a long period of 'bad press' about curiosity killing the cat, curiosity is now applauded as a much-needed attribute, particularly in a VUCA world. We need to become more curious about our own behavioural responses and capabilities ***along with*** those of the people and world around us.

Being curious is to have a mind that is continuously open to learning and new ideas, which in turn means we pick up more clues and cues to find anchors of certainty. It's critical for an agile mindset, as it demonstrates the flexibility and ability to proactively seek information to help make sense of uncertainty and ambiguity to break new ground. In a recent Harvard Business Review article, Tomas Chamorro-Premuzic writes that curiosity is as important as IQ (Intelligence Quotient) and EQ (Emotional Quotient), labelling the virtue as CQ for Curiosity Quotient.

Our brains love to be curious, as we are hardwired to file and recall new experiences and information. When you continue to learn, you build new neural pathways, keeping your mind active and agile. Discovery is exciting and the curious brain is rewarded with new information, such as when you have an 'aha' moment, where you get that insight or epiphany. Neuroscientist David Rock explains that when we solve a problem through a flash of inspiration, our brains enjoy a burst of dopamine, the feel-good chemical associated with the 'reward centre' in our brain.

Curiosity helps us to manage complexity, making us more tolerant of ambiguity and leading to deeper knowledge over time, so it is a useful tool for handling complex problems. According to Chamorro-Premuzic, the good news is that CQ can be developed. Curiosity is part of the agile mindset we need to navigate the VUCA environment.

## DESIGN THINKING

In the next chapter, *Thinking by Design*, we'll look at the role of Design Thinking, and how it links to Human-Centred Design (HCD) to promote co-creation and deeper engagement with the people affected by the change, with earlier and more meaningful involvement. Design Thinking is focused on defining the problem before moving onto devising a solution.

After we look at Design Thinking, you will land on a chapter dedicated to 'mindset hacks'. Thanks to recent discoveries in brain science, we now know a great deal more about how our mind works, how our mindset and capacity is not fixed, and how we can tweak and optimise this wonderful potential that is there for all of us to enjoy!

As mentioned in the previous chapter, Design Thinking is an *emerging capability* and a *mindset* that enables us to take a deeper human-centred application to our change approach.

It's one of the new capabilities to complement our existing ones. We're now leading and managing change in a disruptive environment, fraught with complexity and ambiguity.

To quote Tim Brown, author of *Change by Design* and CEO of IDEO, Design Thinking is defined as:

*A discipline that uses the designer's sensibility and methods to match people's needs with what is technologically feasible and what a viable business strategy can convert into customer value and market opportunity.*

It's worth pointing out that Design Thinking is often misunderstood to be a practice exclusively associated with art and design. The word 'design' can suggest that there is an artefact completed at the end of the process. In Design Thinking, the end result is not always a physical artefact, as one might expect an art and design student to produce.

Design Thinking is a framework that opens deep engagement with the end user, where the end result may be a tangible product or something less tangible, such a new or revised service offering. It's a way of thinking that starts with the customer or end user.

## DESIGN THINKING AS A CAPABILITY

Taking into account Tim Brown's definition of Design Thinking, I've broadly defined the capability, in a change context, as:

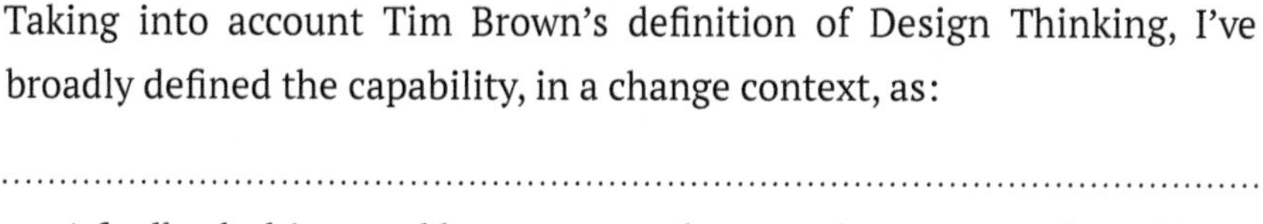

*A feedback-driven and human-centred approach to create a desirable future for employees and customers.*

It means to put our biases aside, and spend time defining the problem to co-create a solution from a holistic perspective that involves and considers the end user. It combines both divergent and convergent thinking to explore all possibilities and then narrow them down to the agreed solution. Starting with divergent thinking, the objective is to generate as many ideas as possible, followed by convergent thinking to narrow them down and identify the preferred option. This approach makes it a quintessential people-centred practice.

A description of Design Thinking isn't complete without an introduction to IDEO. Established in 1991, USA-based IDEO helps organisations innovate and grow using human-centred, design-based practices for product and service development. IDEO has won numerous awards with global reach through working with organisations such as Apple, Coca-Cola, Ford and Air New Zealand.

### *How it connects to Human-Centred Design*

The terms *Design Thinking* and *Human-Centred Design* (often seen abbreviated to HCD) are often used interchangeably. You may see these terms associated with User Experience (UX), Customer Experience (CX), customer-centricity and systems thinking. Because a solution or new product usually translates to change, this is now a much-needed capability for leading and managing change.

Part of developing an agile mindset, is to apply the Human-Centred Design lens to how we plan for and implement change. It means we are open to new insights from our users and customers, and prepared to consider a range of possibilities. It relies on a great deal of curiosity and a beginner's mindset that is comfortable with *not knowing* the answers. But before we go into the *how*, let's take a closer look at *what* Design Thinking is.

## A CRASH COURSE IN DESIGN THINKING

Design Thinking helps us create a human-centric culture of innovation and transform insights into experiments that potentially become actionable ideas. Overall, it's about defining a problem to design a solution or product with the user in mind. The key principle is that the people who face the problems, or use the product, are the ones who can provide the most relevant insights and solutions.

*Design Thinking is as much about problem defining as it is about problem solving.*

Stanford's Institute of Design, called *d.school*, has developed a Design Thinking process that occurs in five *iterative* steps:

**1** | Empathise

**2** | Define

**3** | Ideate

**4** | Prototype

**5** | Test

Let's take a closer look at each of these five steps to find out:

**1** | What it means,

**2** | How to apply it, and

**3** | What you can do as a #changehack for most of these steps.

### *Step 1: Empathise*

#### *What it means*

In the first step, ***empathise,*** we look for insights about the people for whom we are designing a product or service, or delivering change.

#### *How to apply it*

We learn about our users by watching them, engaging with them and immersing ourselves in their day-to-day life to understand their emotions. To uncover the problem, we listen to their stories, their pain points and their overall views. To immerse ourselves, we need to try to 'walk a mile in their shoes'. This step is also referred to as *immersion* or *discovery.*

The information is often captured in a ***persona***. The persona is a tool to help us learn more about our users. It's a *composite character* profile developed primarily for the purpose of improving the end user experience. A composite character is fictional, but draws on several real characteristics, rather than one typical customer or user. As customer expectations are becoming higher, clever businesses are responding by developing customer-centric approaches in their product and service development. This means your persona is partly fictional and partly real and considers *demographic* characteristics along with *psychographic* ones.

Another tool to investigate customer and user perspectives is an ***empathy map***. This map is often represented in quadrants to capture emotions, pain points, gains and what the users are typically saying and doing *in their environment*. Another section I often add to empathy maps is space to prompt thinking on current and emerging trends and how these may influence the way the end user will experience the product or service.

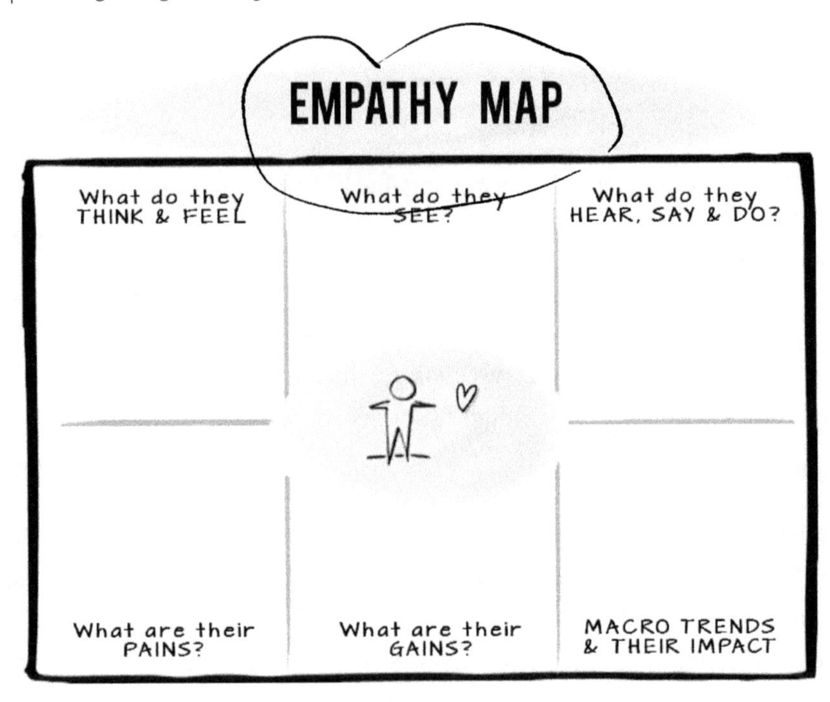


### *#changehack 3 – develop personas of your end users*

For change initiatives, develop end user personas to represent your *impacted employees*. Include demographic elements such as age, gender, life cycle stage, where they live, along with psychographic segmentation such as social preferences and lifestyle choices. In a work context, this would extend to work preferences, such as works part-time, and works remotely.

Professionally built personas rely on extensive demographic and psychographic research to define an organisation's target market. Once patterns are identified after a series of one-on-one interviews, researchers or in-house interviewers will report on behaviours, motivation and attitude, to provide rich data for your development. If your organisation has invested in the preparation of customer personas, be sure to tap into that information for change initiatives that impact external customers, and for changes where your impacted employees may need to adjust their interaction with these customers.

The objective of the persona is to make our users more real and less ambiguous. It improves customer empathy, as we have a 'person' to help us understand behaviour patterns and needs.

Give each persona a name so he/she has an identity that resonates with the team.

Here's an example of a persona I used when developing the content for a workshop on hacking for agile change.

## PERSONA

### CHELSEA CHANGELING

**BACKGROUND**

- Change manager
- Works in the Central Business District (CBD) at the same company for four years
- Married with two children
- Started career in Human Resources, then worked as Change Analyst and was promoted to Change Manager

**DEMOGRAPHICS**

- Skews female
- Manager role
- Age 35
- Lives in suburban Melbourne

***"I'd like to understand what I need to do as a Change Manager, when working on an agile project."***

**IDENTIFIERS**

- Works as part of a project team
- Project managers in organisation are heading off to 'scrum training'
- Uses a well-known and respected global change methodology
- Many projects in the organisation are using a hybrid approach, i.e. waterfall and agile
- Is required to adopt agile practices in her change role, yet is unclear about what exactly that means

Many organisations bring their personas to life by using mannequins or creating life-size cardboard cut-outs of them, which appear in a prominent place to remind us of who we are designing a solution for. I've been in project meetings where we've discussed solutions and change interventions, looked at our personas, and asked ourselves in the group:

- And what would Brigitte (Persona 1) think of that?
- How is Steve (Persona 2) likely to react?

### *Step 2: Define*

#### *What it means*

To ***define*** is to create a point of view that captures our insights on our users' needs: their point of view. We look for patterns that help us develop a problem statement or challenge to identify opportunities. This becomes the focal point for the next step where we ***ideate***.

#### *How to apply it*

Take your persona on a journey. Whether or not you compile a persona of your end-users or customers, there is great value in scheduling time with your users to compile behavioural data using a ***journey map***. This helps *define* a point of view: what your people are complaining about or fearing. What are their pain points in the current state? And how do you hope they will feel in the future state? We are looking to identify patterns in behaviour.

The difference between a ***journey map*** and an ***empathy map***, is that the journey map explores greater detail by capturing the information in the phases of the user experience.

#### *#changehack 4 - run a journey workshop*

The user journey is a visual map, inspired by a customer journey map, to capture end user experiences and perspectives at all steps and touchpoints with your change initiative.

You don't need a persona to run a journey workshop, as you will also have impacted and interested parties in the room. Agree on the relevant phases or touchpoints for your change initiative.

Develop the visual journey with your impacted users and stakeholders to map the *current* state. When I run the journey workshop, I prepare this flipchart on butcher's paper:

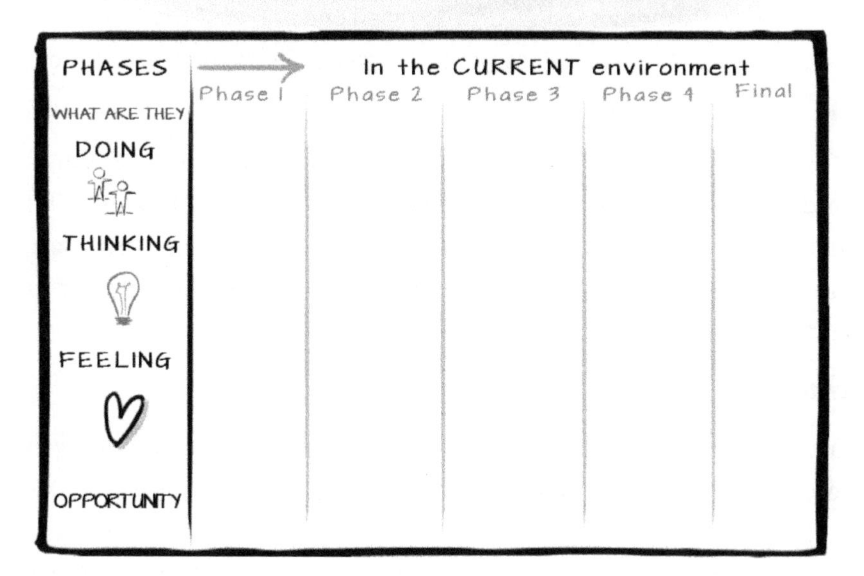


This map records how they are feeling *now* about their current state and ways of working, along with what they are thinking and doing *now*. Document their actions, thoughts and feelings for each phase of their interaction with the work flow, which brings their experience to life. Record all pain points and discuss opportunities on how these can be improved.

You will be able to use the content from your current state journey map to help you build your change impact assessment as well.

### Step 3: Ideate

#### What it means

At the ***ideate*** step, we brainstorm to uncover a range of creative solutions to the problems and opportunities identified in the journey map, with suspended judgement. There are some ideation tips later in this chapter.

#### How to apply it

Ideation is about generating ideas to leverage divergent thinking and to challenge expected solutions. No doubt you've run or participated in numerous brainstorming sessions. Try to recall one or two of those sessions and think about how your ideas were recorded, or listened to. Which were the more successful brainstorms, and why?

Be aware of your mindset. When we meet to gather ideas, we bring with us our experiences and preconceived ideas; in other words, our biases. Our experiences can be both a blessing and a curse. Whilst we bring great ideas through our personal lens, it's incredibly hard to suspend judgement so we can simply observe without passing comment.

#### #changehack 5—cook up an idea storm

Now that the innovation bar keeps being raised, we need to become even more creative and take our brainstorming sessions to a new level, to ideate:

- Defer judgement - there are no *good* or *bad* ideas. You can narrow them later. Remember the beginner's mindset discussed in the last chapter?
- Encourage all wild and woolly ideas - even if they appear unrealistic. A wild idea may prompt another less extreme one.
- Respect - one conversation at a time to give everyone a voice.
- Visual - encourage people to draw their ideas, even if only in stick figures.
- Go for quantity over quality to get started. A tip I hear from design thinkers is to ask your team to set a goal of how many

ideas they can generate in a predetermined time frame. Watch them beat it every time!

### Step 4: Prototype

#### What it means

When we ***prototype***, we experiment by putting together a model or representation of the ideas to show others. Sometimes referred to as *rapid prototyping*, this is an inexpensive prototype with a *fail fast, learn fast* approach. We present it back to our users and/or customers to gather feedback and to narrow or fine-tune options.

#### How to apply it

A prototype can be a storyboard, a rough sketch, a wall of post-it notes or a visual canvas. A clever prototyping technique is *bodystorming* - a process where the end users role-play as if they are in the future state. The purpose is to have something in draft form in front of us to drive a conversation with the end users you've already engaged, and look for what won't work. In this step, you can test more than one idea.

#### #changehack 6 – show the future state in a journey map

Based on the information you've gathered in your journey map of the current state with opportunities in the *define* phase, and ideas from the *ideate* phase, draw a journey map using the same template as before, to play back to your end users.

Once discussed with your users, this visual capture of the future state will also inform your change impact assessment.

### Step 5: Test

#### What it means

***Testing*** is the time to refine the solution. Don't be surprised if this step leads to further iterations or takes you back to earlier steps to redefine and find out more about your users.

*How to apply it*

Test this with a new user group, and walk them through the prototype as though they are your first users. This further tests the improved version of your prototype that has considered the feedback gathered.

Depending on the change initiative being introduced, this step could involve revisions to a storyboard or visual canvas, a simulator environment, or a pilot workshop. The testing step may even take you back to the empathy map or journey map as you may gain new insights.

## MORE TIPS ON JOURNEY MAPPING

There are many ways to use the journey mapping approach to deepen engagement and co-create solutions. The workshops also initiate conversations with stakeholders and impacted employees, to plan change actions leading up to implementation.

You can use the journey workshops to ask employees what they want to see take place before implementation to support adoption, so a collaborative approach starts early in the change planning. This creates a mental picture of the change initiative for your users and provides early insights in three ways:

1 | What they are DOING now, and what they see themselves DOING

2 | What they are THINKING now, and how they would like to THINK

3 | What they are FEELING now, and how they would like to be FEELING.

Make sure that the journey maps you draw are visible and top of mind in your project discussions and planning, as you will continue to reference these insights. Make them available as iterative, 'live' documents that can be updated by your users.

The journey workshop will save a great deal of time later by identifying your user's most important touchpoints. The added benefits are:

- Early engagement - gets people on the same page
- Valuable information for change impact assessments and change plans
- A picture of the desired state for end users
- Clues on what success will look like
- As a visual, it's easy to understand, share and update.

By asking employees what they see themselves doing, along with how they want to feel, and what they want to think after an implementation, means we are asking them to play a meaningful role in imagining a successful future state. This involvement through future-pacing prepares people for the change with visual imagery. It engages them in what success looks like, giving them a positive view of the new world. The key benefit for change practitioners is that we gain insights into what a desired future state looks like from a user's perspective.

## WHERE DESIGN THINKING MEETS CHANGE MANAGEMENT

Applying the Design Thinking lens sharpens our focus to the people side of our change practice, taking us back to the very heart of what we do: help our people adopt the change. With this view, Design Thinking becomes a valuable part of our toolkit when developing change plans, and a capability we need to build. In doing so, we're demonstrating to our clients and project teams that we're aligning our capability and value as change leaders and professionals to the changing demands of the business environment.

The Design Thinking approach helps us discover, define, review and iterate our change approach with the user experience in mind. Spending time at the beginning to identify the people issues, the experience *now* and what it *could be* helps us identify post-implementation metrics.

Whilst Design Thinking is often applied for customer personas and developing empathy for our customers, we can see the value of applying the same approach to introduce change. Considering our impacted employees as our internal customers provides deep insights and drives meaningful conversations with our stakeholders and impacted people.

An important benefit for change practitioners is that when you apply Design Thinking practices, such as running workshops on journey maps, you create a safe place for people to talk about feelings and thoughts.

*It legitimises a conversation about emotions that may not occur otherwise.*

Now that I've used Design Thinking practices in my change approach, I can't imagine doing it any other way.

***Putting it all together***

Here's a summary of the Design Thinking steps, with a column on what the change leader or practitioner can do, as change hacks and/or artefacts. The activities that appear in italics are the ones I used when designing and developing a new two-day workshop for change professionals.

| | Step | Activity | Role of change leader/ practitioner |
|---|---|---|---|
| 1 | EMPATHISE | Observe and engage.<br>Carry out people-centred research and immersion.<br>Use this discovery process to ask:<br>*Who is my audience?*<br>*What matters to them?* | Gather insights to find out more about your users.<br>Shadow - a day in the life of...<br>*Develop user persona/s.*<br>*Ask them to help you build the persona/s.*<br>Do an empathy map. |

| | Step | Activity | Role of change leader/ practitioner |
|---|---|---|---|
| 2 | **DEFINE** | Create a point of view (PoV) based on user needs.<br><br>Map the user's end-to-end experience. | *User journey map to show the current state process on what the end users are:*<br>• *Doing*<br>• *Thinking*<br>• *Feeling.* |
| 3 | **IDEATE** | Idea storming.<br><br>Challenge expected solutions. | *Lean Coffees (in Chapter 12).*<br><br>*Workshops.*<br><br>*Incubators.*<br><br>*Think tanks.* |
| 4 | **PROTOTYPE** | Narrowing of ideas to take one or two to a physical realm.<br><br>Make it, show it, refine it.<br><br>Be prepared to fail fast, learn fast - gather feedback.<br><br>Playing out what the experience might look like. | Storyboard/story/sketching.<br><br>Future state role play, body-storming.<br><br>User journey map to the future or proposed process on what the end users will be:<br>• Doing<br>• Thinking<br>• Feeling.<br><br>*Visual Management, such as a Change Canvas or Change roadmap.*<br><br>Develop pilot workshop content. |
| 5 | **TEST** | Produce a low-resolution artefact based on insights.<br><br>Test it, show it, refine it again.<br><br>Learn from response/s. | Sandpit testing.<br><br>Playback to users, as if they are your first users.<br><br>*Pilot workshop.*<br><br>*Retrospective at end of pilot workshop with participants.* |

There's a great deal more on design thinking out there. IDEO, Frog Design and Stanford *d.school* have great resources on their websites, referenced at the end of this book, among many more.

© Lena Ross, 2016

Design Thinking, as a human-centred practice, is used to define problems to develop innovative solutions to everyday business challenges.

So you could say that where design thinking meets change management is a real ***sweet spot!***

We've explored what an agile mindset looks like, with a growth mindset, a beginner's mindset with curiosity and resilience, while embracing ambiguity and design thinking. We could say agile mindset mastery is about being open to new ideas and adapting to a fast-paced changing world.

It's the mindset we need for relentless and continuous change.

Pretending or hoping the pace of change and new ways of working will just go away is not an option. We know change is continuous and relentless, just as the D- word is (disruption, there it is...I had to say it!), and is not going on holidays anytime soon.

It's the agile mindset that opens a pathway to numerous opportunities for you personally and professionally.

## WHY WE NEED MINDSET HACKS

The workplace of the future is demanding a different approach to navigate an environment fraught with complexity and ambiguity. The speed at which we are expected to learn, source information and get things done relies on an unprecedented agility in mindset as well as practice. We hear a lot about the need for a growth, learning mindset. But where to start?

Here are three practical mindset hacks we can use straight away to learn, unlearn and relearn, to adopt an even more effective way of thinking for our professional and personal development.

We know that if we keep on doing what we've always done, we will get what we've always got. So let's do something different to change it. Let's hack!

### *Hacking away*

The good news is that you can make changes to your thinking. We know that we can develop and nurture a growth mindset, so everyone can learn to be agile. Phew! So our mindset isn't set in stone. Now, that's a relief!

Even better news is that you don't need formal training or expensive courses to do these. These three *mindset hacks*, that I also call *the three powers,* are not difficult to master; but they do require some discipline, and motivation to apply them. The first step is being aware of them; and with new insights from brain science, we have evidence of how effective they are, which helps with the motivation to try them out.

As contemporary philosopher, Eckhart Tolle, said:

***'Awareness is the greatest agent for change.'***

Here are the three powers with proven success:

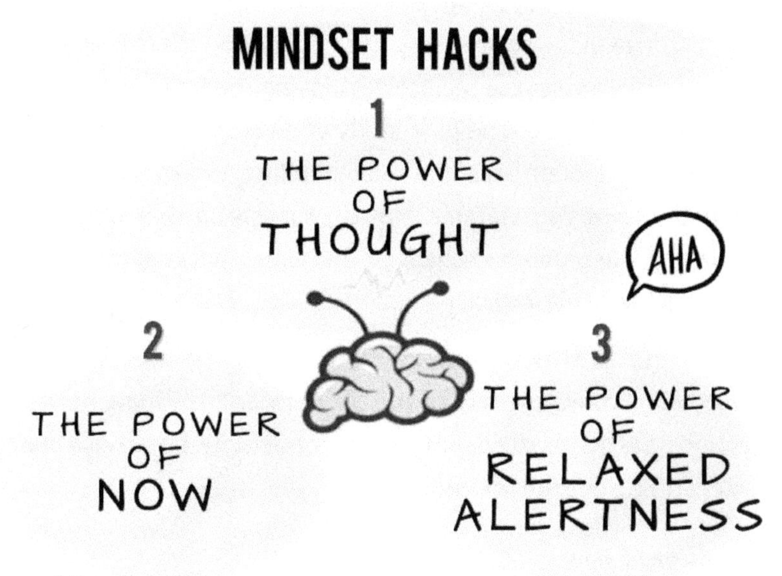


### 1. *The power of thought*

Can we rewire or change our brains? Yes, we can!

The field of neuroplasticity assures us that we can rewire parts of our brain. Based on current fossil evidence, the physiology of our brains hasn't changed in over 200,000 years,. Our neural pathways within that structural physiology are, however, constantly changing.

Imagine our neural pathways as roads. The freeways and highways process ongoing, frequent information and activity. New activity can create a traffic jam on that existing highway, often demanding a new road. Eventually, with repetitive activity, and even thoughts, a new road is formed. By continually bedding down neural messages, that new pathway becomes a more defined highway, allowing greater speed and traction.

This neural pathway concept is explained in a story about piano players. Harvard University carried out research on two groups; both had never played the piano before and were of the same intellect. One group was asked to practise piano scales every day for a period of time. The second group was asked to visualise themselves playing the same piano scales for the same period of time. The post-study brain scans revealed very interesting results. The brain area that relates to finger movements of BOTH groups had shown considerable growth; the group that only thought about playing the piano had changed the same neural pathways as the group that actually played the piano.

So a new chord is struck when we ask people to change or learn new things, as we're asking them to rewire their brains by forming new neural connections. The key is to not only repeat the activity, but to also imagine yourself carrying out the activity.

### 2. *The power of now*

To be aware of now is to be in the moment and mindful. ***Mindfulness*** is described as *a form of meditation, focusing awareness on the present moment, our breath, our thoughts and surroundings.* Mindfulness also has the capacity to change the neural pathways in our brain.

In the chaotic *busy-ness* of our lives where we are accessible around the clock, we rarely pause in our waking moments. This is no surprise because our brains process up to 50,000 thoughts each day.

When we are mindful, we also create the capacity to 'label' our emotions. This is a particularly useful practice to catch ourselves when we respond with feelings of anger or surprise to an event or new information. When we pause to label an emotion, it helps regulate our response. It lowers the activity in the *amygdala*, which is the emotional centre of our brain. When we hear new information, it's likely we may perceive this as threat, putting our amygdala into high gear.

As the emotional centre in our brain, the amygdala regulates the flight, fight or freeze response. Under threat, it responds irrationally. As a survival mechanism, the amygdala acts as a 'gateway' to new stimuli and processes information before it is sent to the 'rational brain'. New information triggers an error signal in our brain, which creates an emotion of fear and anxiety. You may have heard this emotional outburst referred to as the 'amygdala hijack' – a term coined by Daniel Goleman, author of bestselling book *Emotional Intelligence.*

This part of the brain literally saps energy from the rational part of our brain, reducing logical thinking. Neuroscientists estimate that when we experience an 'amygdala hijack', we reduce our IQ by 10 to 15 points!

By labelling, we improve our self-awareness and reduce the impact of this shut-down effect in the brain when we experience the amygdala hijack. It's been proven that by stopping and labelling our response, we draw conscious awareness to what is otherwise a sub-conscious process. No wonder this mindful practice is often positioned as:

*If you can name it, you can tame it!*

We can see that being mindful has many benefits. It can calm our minds and reduce stress and anxiety, resulting in a positive physiological effect on the brain.

### #changehack 7 - schedule me-time

This is a hack for yourself:

- Schedule time out - just as you would for any other activity or meeting, to pause and focus on the now. Be equally mindful of the benefits.
- Spread the word - tell other people how you have become calmer through this practice and they should try it.
- Explore the many apps you can download to help you be more mindful.

### *3. The power of relaxed alertness*

Training professionals who practise accelerated learning principles recognise that Alpha is a useful brain wave state to stimulate creativity and help learners synthesise new information. According to the Bulgarian educational psychologist Dr Georgi Lozanov, the Alpha brain wave is the most receptive for learning and for cementing new information into the subconscious. However, these benefits need not be restricted to yoga masters, people who meditate regularly, and experienced trainers. With a little practice and commitment, the Alpha brain wave state can be achieved and enjoyed by anyone.

The Alpha state can be used productively for creative visualisation and restating affirmations to help you overcome negative inner self-talk. Lie back, relax and allow Alpha to help you access your brain's creative potential and intuitive thinking. It's well known that great moments of insight occur when you are in this relaxed state. One of the most famous stories is of Archimedes, the ancient Greek mathematician. The 'problem' that Archimedes needed to solve was to calculate the volume of gold in the king's crown, a solid artefact made up of very odd and numerous shapes. Taking time out for a relaxing bath was the least expected time for his AHA moment. As he stepped into the bath, he noticed that the water level rose. It occurred to Archimedes that the volume of water displaced must be equal to the volume of the item placed in the water.

This moment is famously retold as his 'Eureka' moment, as it's reported that upon his discovery, Archimedes jumped out of the bath and ran down the street shouting 'Eureka' to announce that he had found the solution.

Creating an environment for Alpha brain waves helps you make connections that previously eluded you, for break-through thinking. If you think about moments when you arrived at your best ideas or most creative insights, it's likely they occurred when you've relaxed and stopped applying conscious thought to the issue.

### *#changehack 8 - create an AHA environment*

As a leader, you can provide opportunities for people to discover their own insights. Instead of providing answers, give them the time and space to reach their own 'AHA' moment, which also activates a reward response in the brain. Neuroscience has taught us that at moments of insight we create new pathways, and learning and new behaviours are more likely to stick.

For rewiring to take place, the brain must be engaged and open to learning. This can only occur when the right conditions are in place, with a comfortable, non-threatening learning environment. Reducing or eliminating the threat response also creates the right conditions for people to reach their own solutions, and arrive at their personal moments of epiphany. We learn best, and therefore rewire most effectively, when we feel comfortable and involved.

Alpha is one of four brain wave states, and occurs when the brain generates electrical frequencies between 8 to 13 cycles per second. Compare this to the brain waves of your conscious mind that operate at 13 to 25 cycles per second in the Beta state. In Theta, often associated with the early hours of sleep, our brain operates at 4 to 7 cycles per second. Delta, at only 1 to 3 cycles per second, is what we experience when we are in a deep, dreamless sleep.

*Destination Alpha*

| Brain Wave State | Brain Wave Cycles per second | Characteristics |
|---|---|---|
| Beta | 13–25 | Conscious, awake |
| Alpha | 8–13 | Relaxed alertness |
| Theta | 4–7 | Early hours of sleep |
| Delta | 1-3 | Deeper, dreamless sleep |

Alpha is a peaceful, relaxed, yet focused state of consciousness. In addition to its pleasant state of relaxation, you can enhance your learning and memory when combined with the right music.

### #changehack 9 - power up your playlist

You can get a little help inducing the Alpha state, and it's as simple as downloading the right music tracks on your playlist. Listen to it while you are working or relaxing. I often play baroque and classical music during breaks, moments of reflection and syndicate break-outs in my workshops.

Between the years of 1650 and 1750, Baroque composers set out to create music to lift the spirit and free the mind. When Dr Georgi Lozanov pioneered methods to accelerate learning in 1960, he found that Baroque music has brain boosting power. This rhythmical, soothing music enhances the ability to absorb and remember information. Its steady tempo of around 60 beats per minute parallels the brain's wavelength to a state of 'relaxed alertness', otherwise known as alpha brain wave patterns.

#### *The famous 'Mozart Effect'*

Any discussion on the effects of music on the brain is not complete without some mention of the research carried out at the University of California's Centre for Neurobiology of Learning and Memory in the early 1990s. The studies concluded that a strong link exists between listening to Mozart's music and spatial reasoning. The conclusions suggest that listening to Mozart helps to organise brain functioning, especially creative processes, associated with spatial-temporal reasoning. Mozart's music has been defined as unique in its simplicity and purity of rhythms and melodies, which optimise an atmosphere of harmony. The 'Mozart Effect' lasts only 15 minutes after the music stops.

Whilst classical music was typically composed from 1750 onwards, many pieces are recorded at the same tempo as Baroque music. This makes classical music, and Mozart specifically, equally effective in creating an auditory environment to help learning and revising information.

In his book *Accelerated Learning,* Colin Rose identified that Baroque and Classical music pieces address different learning functions. Whilst Baroque music is ideal for absorbing new information, Classical music is better suited for revision and memory recall. Rose goes on to call this the 'Passive Concert' (Baroque) and 'Active Concert' (Classical).

Below is a table I prepared for an article I wrote for the Australian Institute of Training & Development magazine back in 2000. My absolute favourite is Pachelbel's Canon in D Major.

***Using Baroque and Classical music***

| Music | Period | Composers* | Application |
|---|---|---|---|
| Baroque | 1600-1750 | Vivaldi, Handel, Bach, Pachelbel, Corelli, Telemann, Albinoni | Passive concert<br>• Uptake of new information<br>• Drawing learning maps |
| Classical | 1750 onwards | Mozart, Brahms, Beethoven, Haydn, Tchaikovsky, Schubert, Mendelssohn | Active concert<br>• Reviewing, memorising and revision work, notes, books<br>• Reviewing learning maps |

*List of composers is not exhaustive

For all of us, a better understanding of our brain function helps us improve our performance at individual, team or organisational levels.

These new insights, backed by proven research, have numerous implications:

- In a medical context, there are encouraging results for people recovering from brain injury;
- From a perspective of emotional regulation, we can label and calm our emotional responses, we can relearn and establish new neural pathways and improve our capacity for breakthrough moments;
- Leaders who understand these mindset hacks can model positive behaviours to their teams;
- We can apply the mindset hacks to help us navigate ourselves and others through change.

Knowing we can do this by thoughts alone, armed with these mindset hacks, is empowering!

# HOW YOU ACT

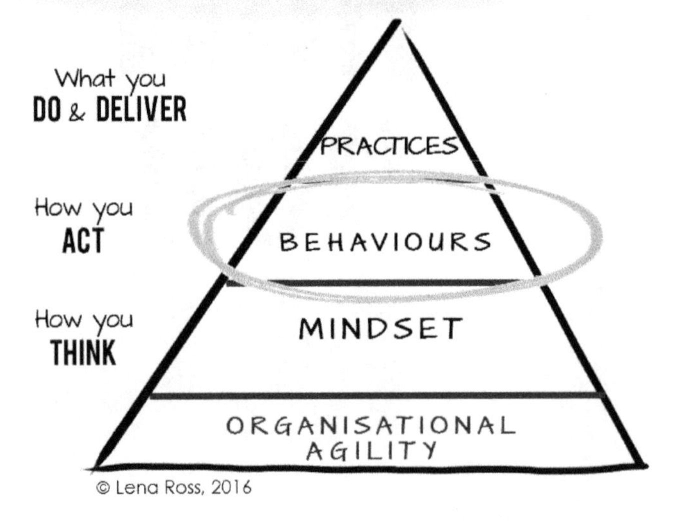
AGILE AS A CAPABILITY
What you
DO & DELIVER
How you
ACT
How you
THINK
PRACTICES
BEHAVIOURS
MINDSET
ORGANISATIONAL
AGILITY
© Lena Ross, 2016

Agile behaviours, at team and individual level, can be broadly described as behaviours that rely on high levels of trust and mutual accountability. The characteristics of collaboration, transparency, honesty, and a willingness to work outside their area of expertise enable team members to be adaptable and continuously improve their practices.

An Agile team is self-organised; it is a group of motivated and proactive individuals who have the authority to make decisions, and don't wait for their leader to assign work. The Agile Principles listed in Chapter 2, *Getting on the Same Page with Agile,* also provide guidance on the behaviours.

Many project managers have recognised the importance of recruiting team members with the 'right' behaviours, and many employ for 'will' (attitude) over 'skill' as skills are easier to teach than new behaviours.

## HOW YOU ACT

Behaviour is *how you act*, making up an important part of the definition of agile as a capability. As a team is made up of a group of individuals, let's firstly take a look at the agile individual.

## THE AGILE INDIVIDUAL

Starting with an agile mindset (of course), the agile individual demonstrates a growth and learning mindset, as explored in an earlier chapter. The behaviours an agile individual will be expected to bring to the team are:

- Collaboration
- Ability to deal with ambiguity
- Adaptability
- Honesty
- Openness to feedback
- Willingness to share knowledge.

Whether we are leading others or not, we need to keep in mind that how we act is noticed and has an impact on others - there is a ripple effect.

### *The ripple effect*

There are a few subconscious behaviours that create a ripple effect when we are around others. As an example, here's a familiar scenario. When we are around people who are negative and constantly complaining, we feel tired and drained. You might even call them emotional vampires. The flip side is that when we surround ourselves with positive, upbeat people, we feel energised. It's no wonder that on some days we are more exhausted than we should be, for no other reason other than the company we've kept.

When this happens, we are experiencing *emotional contagion*, which is defined as the *transfer of moods.*

### *Designed to align*

The reason it's so easy to absorb others' emotions, or even mimic behaviour around us, is that we are hardwired to do so. Mirroring and absorbing the emotions of people around us is an evolutionary survival skill, as it was critical that we harmonised with our tribe. Mirroring is a psychological term to describe the behaviour of subconsciously imitating the characteristics of those around us. As social creatures, we are naturally designed to align to moods and emotions, so we mirror others at a subconscious level. And this takes place with *both* negative and positive emotions.

If you want to watch an amusing clip on how easy it is to mimic the behaviour of people around us, take a look at one of Asch's Conformity Experiments, called the *elevator experiment*. In this experiment, three 'plants' in the group deliberately face the rear of the elevator, whilst one person enters and firstly faces the door. It's not long before the one facing the front of the elevator mimics the others and faces the rear. This reminds us how easy it is for us to conform. The experiment became popular when it appeared on television in the early 1960s in a programme called *Candid Camera* as the 'face the rear' elevator test. You can find this to watch on YouTube.

Don't underestimate the effects of your own actions. When explaining individual behaviour, it's important to be aware that the way we act will have an immediate impact on how our team members and colleagues feel.

***Ask yourself:***

- What emotional footprint do I leave?
- What footprint are my leaders leaving? My peers?
- Am I aware when this is happening to me?
- What can I do about it?

***Tips***

- Spend more time with people who leave you energised and positive.
- If you can't avoid negative people, try to limit your time with them. When I need to meet with a negative person, I schedule a catch-up with a positive colleague afterwards. This approach is especially useful when interacting with difficult stakeholders.
- If you know emotions are contagious, when you are in the company of a negative person, you will be able to identify it. Once you are aware it's happening, smile. Speak calmly. Respond with opposite emotions, with the hope that you will be able to change their mood.
- If someone with negative behaviours is relentless, you may need

to label it for them. Tell them that their approach is negative/aggressive/upsetting and suggest they explore other ways to communicate or work through the issue, especially if you can't help them directly.

Emotional contagion helps us understand the scope of impact one person has on the people around them.

Be the person that leaves people energised, not drained ☺.

## THE AGILE TEAM

When we talk about agile teams, it's often in reference to a project team that is assigned to an 'Agile project'. In this context, you are a change practitioner working on an Agile project. Your project manager is most likely called a *scrum master.*

Let's park this scenario for a moment. Instead, let's look at a broader view of agile behaviours. Behaviours that are valued and identified as critical to the success of an Agile project team *are also behaviours that will serve us well in any project or change assignment.*

### *Key roles*

Before we continue, and as I've just mentioned 'scrum master', let's take a look at the key roles in an Agile team so you are familiar with the terms and responsibilities.

There's a plethora of definitions out there; follow your curiosity and see what you find.

### *Scrum master*

A ***scrum master*** is the team lead, who is defined as the facilitator for an Agile development team. They are responsible for:

- removing obstacles for the team
- acting as servant-leaders to help their teams become accountable for themselves

- putting aside their own ego and desire for status
- helping the team meet their commitments.

### Product owner

As the key stakeholder, or project sponsor, the ***product owner***:

- represents the business or the stakeholders
- acts as the voice of the customer
- is responsible for optimising return on investment.

Where there is a discussion or written material on an Agile team, you are likely to come across the concept of *self-organising.*

### The self-organising team

The concept of self-organising teams, however, is not unique to Agile software development teams. If we define a self-organising team through a broader, social science lens, it's a team that 'can create new approaches and adapt to meet new challenges in their environment'.

This definition suggests agility in the teams themselves, where there is a nimbleness to change direction when required. In the absence of a formal leader, the members of this team are able to organise themselves, to manage and respond to external disturbances and hiccups, and quickly refocus on the task at hand.

There is a misconception that these teams are completely autonomous to do what they want. Esther Derby, Agile coach and consultant, has written many blogs on this topic setting this misconception straight by describing self-organising teams as those that need goals and effective leaders to create a supportive environment, with appropriate boundaries.

### What does a self-organising team actually look like?

The challenge with self-organising teams is that the concept goes against formal and conventional leadership practice. This demands a shift from 'command and control' hierarchical management styles, which is a significant behaviour shift in itself for many leaders. From looking at emotional contagion, we know that the leader's behaviour will set the tone for how the rest of the team responds and performs.

To lead a self-organising team is to empower and trust your team members. This means putting aside status and control to provide more autonomy for faster decision making. Make it a safe environment to experiment and try again, by sending a clear message that mistakes are valuable lessons. Empowering team members may result in a few bumps at first, and may even result in some not-so-favourable actions and decisions while team members are not familiar with such autonomy. Longer term, the autonomy will enable professional growth, unleash potential and most likely promote a level of motivation to keep the team members energised.

### *Small things CAN make a big difference*

While this sounds like a tough challenge to get a few things right - such as the leadership, the level of autonomy, the trust - we can see how important it is to recruit and reward the desired behaviours. If you are a team leader, or asked to create a self-organising team, don't forget that team bonding sessions go a long way in building relationships, trust and open dialogue. I won't forget one tough project I worked on where every Friday morning, our project lead blew a whistle, asked us to stop what we were doing and join him in the kitchen area for muffins and a round of trivia questions.

### *What else makes an Agile team different?*

Much has been written about the core values of an Agile project team. Scrum masters learn these principles in their training and then (hopefully) model and encourage the behaviours in their practice.

The expected behaviours are described in a blog by expert scrum master and blogger, Christian Miles, as he defines the five core values of Scrum:

- Focus
- Courage
- Openness

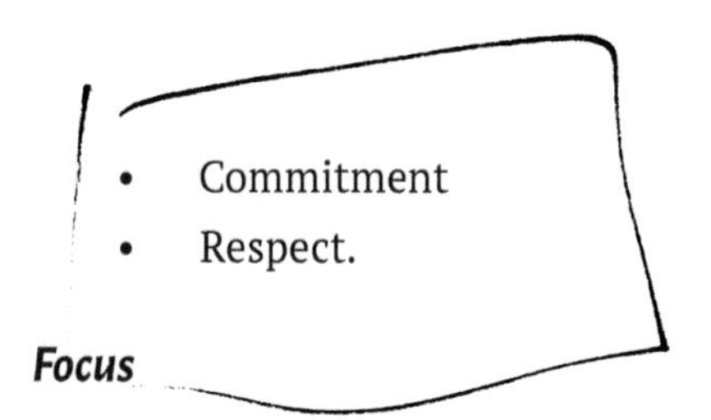

- Commitment
- Respect.

### *Focus*

Agile practices such as Kanban boards and stand-up meetings provide focus to the agile team. On an Agile project, the scrum master (team lead) removes distractions to help the team focus on delivery.

### *Courage*

To be brave is to experiment with new ideas and practices, to be ready for challenges and shifting priorities, and to speak out respectfully. The scrum master needs to demonstrate courage when engaging with stakeholders and the product owner.

### *Openness*

Provide transparency about the state of the project as well as about the progress of your own work. This relies on a climate of trust, where there is no fear of being honest or trying new things. There is no fear of reporting on the true progress of your work to stakeholders or peers, or asking for help if needed.

### *Commitment*

Commitment to each other as team members and to delivery of the solution. This means team members will complete what was agreed in the way it was agreed it would be completed. To deliver the solution, may require team members to work outside their own expertise area to help others meet this commitment.

### *Respect*

Each team member will bring personal strengths and weaknesses to the team. There must be respect for teams and individuals, including those working remotely, or in other parts of the organisation. This also means the scrum master and the product owner demonstrate respect for each other's responsibilities.

We can see the behaviours are difficult to separate from mindset. It takes an agile mindset that's open to learning and feedback to be an agile-friendly team member.

### *#changehack 10 - get the right people on board*

Have you noticed that in looking at agile mindset and behaviours, there has been no reference to the core capabilities required of the change practitioner or change leader?

We can see that an agile mindset and agile-aligned behaviours are critical success factors to establish any team that will thrive and perform well in a disruptive environment.

When looking for new team members, we need to align our questions and search approach to uncover these characteristics in individuals. Depending on the actual skill set the project needs, the recruiting manager may consider hiring for WILL as well as SKILL.

The notion of selecting people based on WILL and SKILL is beautifully expressed as the Will/Skill Matrix. This matrix is one of my favourite models made popular in the book *The Tao of Coaching* by Max Landsberg. The matrix is a tool to help leaders determine the most effective coaching approach they should apply, depending on the team member's motivation and capability.

When you think of your employees in terms of *will* and *skill*, you will start thinking of a few things:

- How likely are they to complete the task based on their skill?
- How much do they want to complete the task?
- What is my best approach when they are skilled?
- What is my best approach when their motivation is low?

Imagine you have just recruited two new team members. Your first recruit has a great deal of experience in Agile teams and has attended a few courses on Agile practices. But when you watch him/her interact with the rest of the team, you notice the behaviours are not aligned. This recruit has already upset other team members with their brash manner and reluctance to accept feedback. This person is high in skill and low in will.

You were a bit hesitant to appoint your second recruit. They came highly recommended from another large organisation, yet had less experience in Agile practices than you hoped. This person demonstrates a learning mind and is keen to try new things and help out team members. By contrast, this person is lower in skill, but likely to be higher in will.

Now, as a leader, you will take different approaches to develop these two employees. But which team member will you prefer to coach?

If you can hire someone HIGH in both - well done you! When recruiting candidates, I tend to favour *will* over *skill*, as experience has taught me that someone with a learning mindset is often more open to coaching than someone with low motivation. It's no surprise that a team member with LOW skill and LOW will is one who should be exiting!

## POWER IS CHANGING

On the topic of agile behaviours, it's interesting to make note of how power is shifting in organisations. As we know, the ways we are working are changing, so it's no surprise that the distribution of power, and how power is exercised in a business environment, are also shifting. There are several external forces driving the shifts in power base - globalisation, generational skews towards millennials, digitalisation, multiple generations in the workplace, technology, and mobility, to name a few that are shaping the future of work.

In his TED talk titled '*What new power looks like*', Jeremy Heimans used the following table to summarise the key trends.

There are similar-looking tables circulating that represent old thinking/ new thinking.

| OLD POWER | NEW POWER |
| --- | --- |
| CURRENCY | CURRENT |
| HELD BY FEW | HELD BY MANY |
| DOWNLOADS | UPLOADS |
| COMMANDS | SHARES |
| LEADER-DRIVEN | PEER-DRIVEN |
| CLOSED | OPEN |

**SOURCE:** Jeremy Heimans' TED Talk (2014): *What new power looks like*

The message here is clear. Traditional, hierarchical models of power with command and control leadership are no longer hitting the mark in motivating the masses. Command and control is being replaced by connection and collaboration. Information, the commodity that was once restricted and served as a power base for senior executives, is now easier to access and share. Power and status are being disrupted, and agile behaviours are right for these new ways of leading, engaging and communicating with our teams.

*New power* is built on trust and sharing of knowledge. If we contrast this with positional power and centralised knowledge, we can see that information is no longer distributed via a vertical stream, from the top down, as a cascaded approach. New ways of working, such as the open-plan office and Enterprise Social Networks, are enabling the shift. Massive Open Online Courses, known as MOOCs, are social networks that are brilliant examples of how knowledge is now available at low or no cost, anytime, anywhere, to anyone.

### *What does this mean for change delivery?*

With these shifts occurring in the workplace, and decentralisation of formal power, it's time for the change practitioner to re-think:

- engagement models
- participatory communication approaches over the cascade model of one-way top-down
- where people will go for information
- how people are influenced - who are the 'new' influencers?

This means we need to explore different ways to communicate and engage - leading us to the next chapter on *Communicate to Co-create.*

And if you've noticed that the table on Old Power/New Power reads a little bit like the difference between an agile team and a conventional project team, you are spot on!

In a time and place where power is being redefined and shifting, the way we communicate and influence is changing. As change practitioners and leaders, we need to tap into new and different communication channels to achieve two key objectives:

**1** | To inform

**2** | To engage.

These new channels are considered disruptive because they differ from the power-based and top-down approaches. This is related to behaviour, as it relies on characteristics mentioned in the last chapter - collaboration, adaptiveness and transparency. So here are more ways in which small things can make a big difference.

A conventional change communication plan relies on top-down communication, which is one-way, and often delivered by a senior employee who has formal influence and power in the organisation. This type of communication continues to play a role in communicating change to *inform* and to demonstrate endorsement of and support for the initiative. Rarely, however, does it invite feedback or engagement.

Participatory two-way communication both *informs* and *engages* the audience. It invites conversation and creates opportunity for involvement and co-creation. And what a great way to uncover your potential change advocates!

## REACHING OUR AUDIENCE

If we also take into account the overwhelming amount of information we receive and process each day, we need a few hacks and some creativity to make sure our messages are reaching our audience. There are over 17,500 blog posts alone on the topic of email overload. We know it's a reality. Every change leader and practitioner has their own communications approach, with a range of proven communication channels. So how does your message get the cut-through?

## CHANNELS FOR CO-CREATION

We need additional ways to complement our communications toolkit. The way to build on our suite of proven channels is to leverage disruptive and agile approaches. There are three approaches to explore as communication channels for co-creation. Each channel is a change hack in itself.

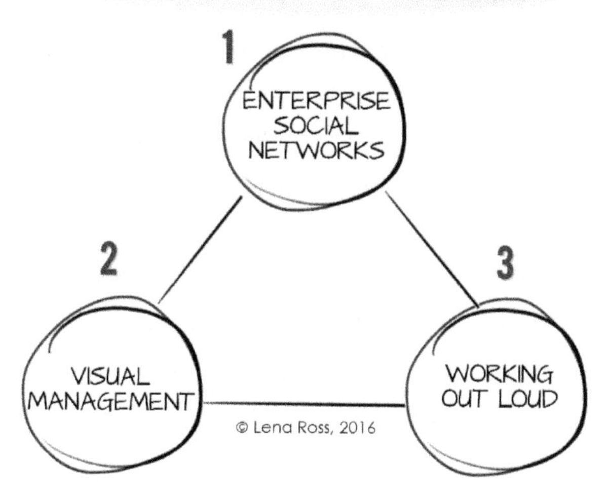

### 1. *Enterprise Social Networks (ESNs)*

An Enterprise Social Network (ESN) is a platform used in organisations to facilitate online communication and collaboration. A leading ESN used in the workplace is Microsoft-owned Yammer. If you're not already familiar with ESNs such as Yammer, think of them as a Facebook for the workplace. If you are of the mindset that an ESN is not a formal communication channel, it's time to watch business trends. It's the *informality* of ESNs that make them effective and a must-have in your toolkit.

Don't be fooled by the word 'social' in Enterprise Social Networks. The collaboration, information exchange and engagement that takes place across business units delivers great value.

In a recent analysis on global ESN trends, it was found that the number of users reached 208 million in 2014, with an expectation of 535 million users by 2018. If we consider the number of GenYs who will enter the workforce over the next couple of years, this is no surprise. This way of collaborating and communicating is a characteristic of the future of work. The most active Yammer group within the corporate platform at one major bank was the Graduate cohort.

#### *#changehack 11 - use your Enterprise Social Network as a change communication channel*

Use your ESN as a communication channel for updates, uploading photographs of visual management boards and events, inviting comments, promoting upcoming events, sharing relevant news articles and your own expertise and knowledge, floating your ideas, crowdsourcing solutions to problems, asking for support or expertise to help you. You can even use Yammer to carry out short online polls for a quick pulse check.

With ESNs come numerous other benefits. They break down silos and geographical barriers, and establish connections across divisions while providing a two-way communication channel that isn't top-down – a real accelerator for co-creation that cannot be overlooked.

ESNs, typically Yammer, are being adopted by more leaders and change practitioners across numerous organisations as critical communication and engagement channels, making them one of the most accessible and effective culture hack tools on hand. In the past, centralised knowledge created a power base, often in the hands of leaders who would decide when to release it. Disruption via Yammer has now dismantled the ivory tower of information and engagement, making knowledge available faster and providing opportunities for everyone to collaborate across divisions, from CEO to the 'shop floor'. Everyone has a voice and an opportunity to be heard and make a difference.

If we refer to the model of Old Power/New Power featured in the last chapter, we can see that channels such as ESNs have disrupted old, formal power. Via ESNs, information is created, shared and distributed by many, rather than being given out in a traditional top-down, cascaded communication.

### *#changehack 12 - get your people on board with Enterprise Social Networks*

Here are some practical tips I've been sharing with my network and on social media, to promote engagement and adoption. These have worked in large organisations when setting up an ESN, such as Yammer, as a channel, or new ESN/Yammer groups:

**1** | Establish a dedicated group for your project/initiative/purpose.

**2** | Enlist the support of your leadership team as they need to role-model ESN.

**3** | Run a couple of lunchtime sessions to 'demystify' your organisation's ESN. Ask attendees to bring their device/s so they can log on and join your group at the session.

**4** | Reward your new adopters quickly with a 'like' and 'reply' or 'share'.

**5** | Include the use of your ESN for social learning and sharing information into your performance measures/scorecards.

**6** | Have a couple of topics/questions related to your field ready to post to provoke discussion, particularly in the early stages of your group's formation, and have some conversation starters ready to post in case things go quiet.

**7** | Back-channel (report back) from events in real time or just after.

**8** | At an event, encourage your participants to report back. Offer an incentive for the first three people who publish a post. In our learning sessions, I build activities into the session that promote Yammer activity and posts, eg search and find activities and posting one key take-away.

**9** | Hashtag your key events and topics to make it a knowledge management tool and for easy search and find later, eg #hackathon, #changeevent2016.

**10** | Promote some offers, eg tickets to an event, that are only available on your ESN.

**11** | Mention it at each employee's point of induction, invite new starters to sign up and join your group.

**12** | When you write an email, refer your readers to an ESN link/thread for more information.

I designed the following diagram to help people understand a typical adoption pattern for social media:

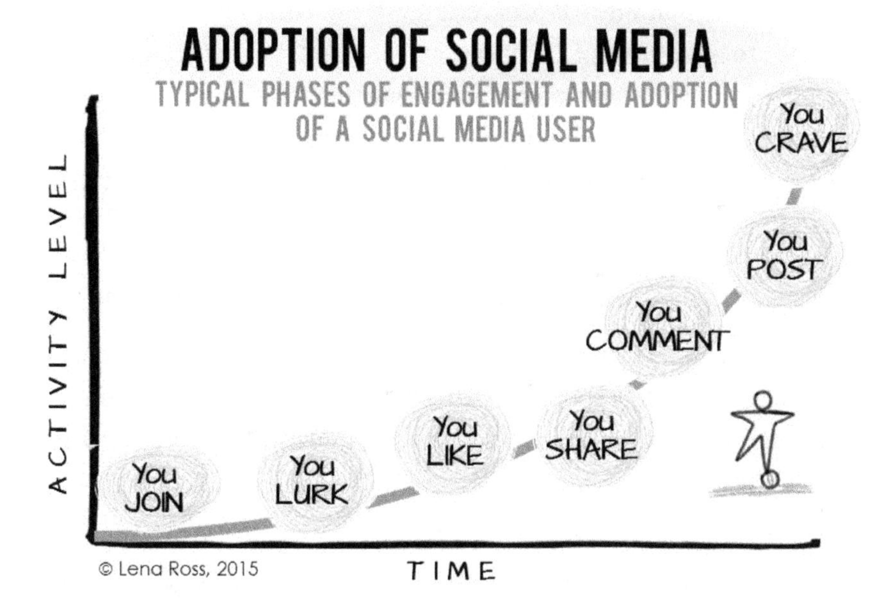


This diagram, with some additional commentary, is available to download as a colour infographic on my website.

## 2. *Visual management*

In John Medina's book, *Brain Rules,* he explores 12 rules for optimising our performance at school, work and home. Among a swag of fantastic tips and information in his work, rule number 10 is 'vision trumps all other senses'.

For too long, we've been inundated by (and inflicted on others) text-based pages of PowerPoint slides. As attention spans become shorter, and we are overwhelmed with mountains of information from various sources, we need to be clever about how we communicate and capture information. It's great if you are already developing visual and engaging slides. Another option is to deliver your key messages via ***infographics***. There are some great infographic packages online where you can experiment with a limited range of templates for free. Look for websites such as *Canva* and *Piktochart* to get started.

Recording information on flipcharts is powerful. There are some messages that need to be delivered or captured in real time. So ***even better*** if you are able to record and deliver information using the power of chunky markers and sheets of paper. The good news is that you don't need to be a gifted artist or calligrapher to create a bit of WOW factor in your presentations and facilitated sessions.

### *#changehack 13 – invest in a one-day course on visual facilitation*

One of the best investments I made was attending a one-day course in visual facilitation. In a short session you will learn tips and tricks on how to optimise the use of your pens and how to quickly draw some very simple, yet effective, icons. You will leave with an 'icon library' and a desire to practise your new skills straight away.

Jump on every opportunity to use your new skill in your personal and professional life. After you attend a session, keep it alive by:

- Building an icon library - look out for simple icons, or search in Google Images, for ideas on what you can collate or re-create;
- Searching 'visual facilitation' or 'graphic recording' in Google Images to see the range of work that's been produced;
- Taking notes visually – when you are in a meeting or listening to a TED talk or lecture.

The benefits of getting visual go beyond improved engagement during your session. Research has shown that information presented with pictures has a recall of 65% after three days, compared with only 10% recall of text-only information.

If our brains were hardwired for a preference of text over pictures, speed reading would be a breeze, and we know it's not easy to learn that art. We know it's impossible to present everything in images in the workplace. When hard data needs to be communicated or recorded, look at options to add the supporting information as an appendix so your key messages remain visual and concise.

What we can do is give some thought to how we can integrate more visuals into our communication so our messages can resonate and be remembered. After all, we want to make an impact and help people enjoy and absorb the new information, let alone actually read our material!

### 3. *Working out loud*

Working out loud (often abbreviated to WOL) is a practice that is growing in popularity due to its simplicity and effectiveness in promoting engagement and co-creation. It's the practice of doing our work in a way that is visible to our colleagues. By working openly, you have the opportunity of gathering additional information and possibly avoiding duplication of effort. How many times have you started research or prepared documentation only to find out later that someone has completed something similar? Something that could have saved you hours of duplicated work? The benefits in working out loud are immediate and easy to see.

WOL is a term first coined in 2011 by Bryce Williams, a social collaboration specialist, when he used it to define work that is observable by others. John Stepper, a WOL advocate, has written numerous blogs and more recently a book on this practice. Stepper has identified five elements to truly define working out loud:

1 | It makes your work visible.

2 | It makes work better – you seek ways to improve your work through feedback and discussion.

3 | It involves leading with generosity – you share your work in progress with others, not just for engagement, but the discussions will help you discover other work underway, and specialist skills you can tap into.

4 | It builds a social network – as you continue to work out loud, you will connect with more like-minded people who are likely to become part of your personal learning network. There is more on developing your learning network in Chapter 17, *So What, Now What?* If you are leading or managing a change, you will find supporters and champions.

5 | It makes your work purposeful – you will identify your purpose and be transparent about it.

I find out interesting and unexpected things when I work out loud. On one occasion, I placed a post on Yammer inviting people to drop into a room I had booked out for a day to see a capability uplift program I was developing. The purpose was to provide visibility and to invite input on the content they were hoping to learn. Because our Yammer group had attracted numerous members outside our immediate team, the post attracted more interest than my initial target group. The result was that by working out loud, I uncovered a broader interest and we were able to join forces with other business units to develop richer content with greater relevance for a larger audience. This prevented what could have been duplication of effort in other business areas. It also introduced diversity of thought. What a great way to hack across organisational silos!

It's a rapid way to gather feedback and invite discussion. People become engaged when they have an opportunity for involvement, and working out loud provides a non-threatening channel for this co-creation. The perfect aid for working out loud is your ESN. This is the fastest and most effective way to announce what you are creating.

### *#changehack 14 - try working out loud*

If you've never tried working out loud, and want to dip in slowly, look out to see if anyone in your organisation is already doing it. If they are, drop in to see them and have a chat about it.

Promote it on your organisation's ESN, or spread the word via email and your team meetings. Book a separate area, such as a meeting room, and assign a timeframe. Be there with an open mind and ready to have great conversations.

For many, working out loud is a step outside their comfort zone, particularly for perfectionists. It means you are showing your work before it's 'fully cooked'. Some fear that the involvement of others may slow them down. The good thing about working out loud is that engagement is invited, not mandatory, so you will attract the people who are interested enough to commit their time to your cause. If you are concerned about too much involvement slowing your progress, set clear expectations about timelines, roles and responsibilities and who owns the final decisions.

Overall, the benefits outweigh any challenges, and it's definitely an approach worth practising that contributes to an open and collaborative culture.

The daily stand-up meeting and the Kanban board are great examples of how an agile team 'works out loud' with their peers.

In these disruptive channels for co-creation, you will see the key themes are ***collaboration*** and ***transparency***. There is less focus on hierarchy and top-down communication and more emphasis on involvement. The communication is two-way, openly inviting discussion and dialogue in real time.

Getting the picture that this approach is aligned with agile behaviours?

# 9 HOW WE ARE HARDWIRED TO BEHAVE

Have you ever wondered about some of the behaviours and responses you've demonstrated over the years, only to be embarrassed by your friends or colleagues asking you what the hell were you thinking at the time? At the time, our response may be an outburst, or a decision may appear sound, yet in hindsight we can't believe the folly of our thinking.

Our primal instincts kick in and often dictate our behaviour at an unconscious level. These instincts link to our work preferences, how we respond to new information and change, along with other behaviours and preferences that transpire in the workplace. Here are a few instincts that are interesting to know when we are hacking for change:

- The ideal team size;
- How we process information;
- Our engagement with rumours and gossip;
- The importance of ritual and ceremony for milestone events.

To further delve into our hardwired behaviour, in the next two chapters we'll also look at:

- How we best learn and retain information;
- The human response to change and new information;

and in the third part on *what we do and deliver:*

- Why storytelling resonates with our hearts and minds.

## PRIMATES AT WORK

As humans, our instincts served us well for hundreds of thousands of years. Our survival behaviours on the savannah often led us to make quick decisions emotionally and impulsively and this bias for survival kept us safe. These primal intuitions and gut feelings in response to threat and survival challenges made the difference between life and death.

On the savannah, our fight/flight response kicked in when we were faced with life threatening events, such as coming into contact with a sabre tooth tiger. In the workplace, the same response is activated by triggers that are not exactly life threatening, such as unexpected email requests and receiving negative feedback on our performance. The survival instincts that served us so well for hundreds of thousands of years, now need to be monitored so our natural responses don't get out of control. There is more detail on our hardwired responses of *threat* and *reward* in Chapter 11 on *The Truth About Resistance*. In the meantime, let's look at what works with our natural preferences.

While we have well and truly evolved in terms of lifestyle, technology and appearance, much of the Stone Age has stayed with us.

Our human behaviour is hardwired and we can use this knowledge of our primal instincts to achieve greater cut-through with our change efforts.

Think of it like this - the primal brain is the hardware, and it is hundreds of thousands of years old. Our twenty-first century digital lifestyle is the software. We're trying to plug this ever-changing new software into a legacy system!

*We really are primates in an office environment.*

Let's take a look at how some of our primal behaviour relates to our modern-day existence, and how we can apply these insights to improve the way we plan and deliver change.

## THE IDEAL TEAM SIZE

How cool would it be to have a number named after you? That's exactly what happened to Oxford evolutionary anthropologist and psychologist, Robin Dunbar. In his extensive research on primates and his fascination with how they spend so much time and effort on social grooming, he came across an interesting social pattern that impacts primates and humans alike. Social grooming is the behaviour where primates and other social animals attend to each other's appearance. For humans, this translates to behaviour such as paying compliments and engaging in small talk. In social media, we groom socially by retweeting and liking posts.

Dunbar discovered that the size of our brains determines the optimal group size we have formed as social creatures. After number-crunching a few complex correlations and ratios between neocortex size, total brain volume and ideal social group size, here's what he came up with for humans as an ideal group size.

The number is 150. This is the number of people with whom we are able to form and maintain stable relationships at one point in time. The world's remaining hunting and gathering clans are made up of around 150 people. Once group membership exceeds 150, the relationships are less meaningful with a diminished sense of connection. If you are keen to start your list, Dunbar's rule of thumb is this – *think about the number of people you would feel obligations towards and would happily do favours for.*

### *The workplace clan: family, village, tribe...*

So if 150 is the maximum number of people with whom we can maintain a trusting relationship, what does this mean when we work in large organisations employing tens of thousands of employees? And what can you do with this information?

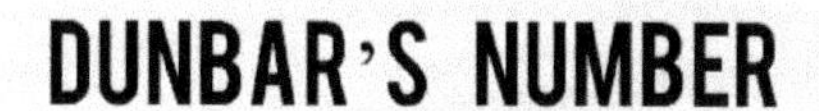


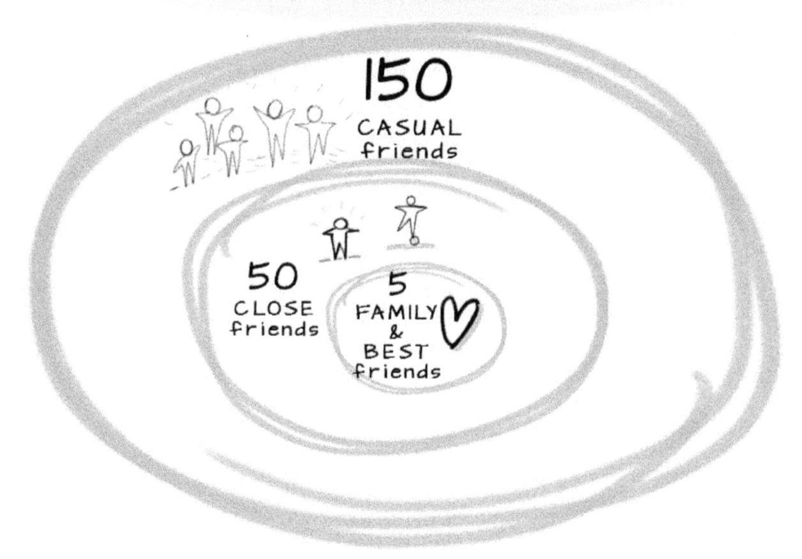


Many companies have already realigned their organisational architecture so their business units or performance units are broken down into teams of 150 or less. For example, Flight Centre has adopted a family-village-tribe operating model that is inspired by Dunbar's thinking and the structure of hunter-gatherer societies. Employees are assigned to small 'units' or teams called families, with a maximum of seven people. The next level is the village with a maximum of 50 people. The next level up is a 'tribe' that is made up of no more than 25 teams, so a tribe is no larger than 150 people. Families of three to seven people (the family unit in Dunbar's model) are accountable for their profit and loss and compete with other families in their tribe.

### *#changehack 15 - consider Dunbar's number in organisational restructures*

Understanding our primal social patterns can point to clues that can make us better in our professional and personal lives.

When changes are being made to business unit realignment, or project teams are being established, we can look for opportunities to follow the Flight Centre model and align team and unit sizes to Dunbar's 'magic' numbers. A large-scale organisation can be made up of numerous units of 150-ish employees, with smaller teams of around 20 people to promote collaboration and optimal social connection. An approach that is intrinsic to our human make-up translates to improved human performance. In turn, improved human performance is linked to better business performance.

## HOW WE PROCESS INFORMATION

### *No more than seven please*

While we are on the topic of numbers and our cognitive capacity, let's look at the number seven. Many moons ago (in the mid-1950s), psychologist George Miller came up with what is now known as Miller's magic number. Through research, he concluded that most adults can retain and recall between five to nine pieces of information in their short-term memory, so the number is seven plus or minus two, making seven the magic number.

The interesting part is that in each of these 'seven plus or minus two pieces of information', it's been found that we can store chunks of information.

### *#changehack 16 - chunk communication so it can be digested*

With limits on our working memory for processing information, we need to keep our communication and learning material simple and easy to follow:

- Use few bullet points, and fewer than nine in any list (the seven +/- two rule)
- Chunk information into these palatable sizes.

## WHY WE LIKE TO GOSSIP

Gossip was critical to early human survival. Firstly, it provided useful information on what worked and what didn't, building on a growing base of oral history. It also provided a channel for strengthening social bonds, as essential activities such as hunting relied on collaboration. Simply put, it's one of the many common behaviours we see in the workplace, as we revert to our primate behaviour.

Robin Dunbar isn't just famous for his number. As he's carried out extensive research on primates, he concluded that gossip is the human version of the social grooming carried out by primates. We've all seen photos or film footage of our primate cousins grooming one another by picking nits and ticks from their coats.

The fact that gossip takes place isn't toxic in itself, unless it's malicious. It's the content and nature of the gossip and rumours that we need to monitor. Organisations are made up of organic and informal communication networks - the invisible networks that lie outside formal hierarchy. Let's work with the notion that gossip and rumours will be part of our professional and personal lives.

In times of uncertainty, when employees are trying to make sense of ambiguity or incomplete information, received through both formal and informal channels, gossip and rumours will flourish. Over-communicating is a typical approach to tackle rumours, but there are some other change hacks we can try.

### *#changehack 17 - tap into grapevines*

- Stay abreast of the rumours - you can uncover a lot from your Enterprise Social Network, such as Yammer. Use this channel to ask what is happening at the water cooler and in the corridors. This opens a two-way communication channel to host and moderate the gossip and to address the rumours.
- Provide face-to-face forums for myth-busting, discussion and FAQs. One way is to add 'myth busting' as a regular team

meeting agenda item. Invite your team to openly talk about the rumours.

- Adopt the agile practice of a Lean Coffee meeting. There's more on this in the next section on *What We Do and Deliver.*
- Following formal face-to-face communication forums, allow time for smaller groups to gather to engage in natural 'gossip'. Ask your team leaders and change champions to circulate and speak with people in these smaller groups, to tap into this grapevine. It's natural to try to fill in the gaps to make sense of uncertainty and gossip. Rumours are one way for people to close this gap.
- If you cannot communicate detail, advise people when details will be confirmed to provide anchor points.
- Set up a rumour or gossip board. Ask your employees to post concerns and rumours on post-it notes on a board. Offer this channel as an anonymous outlet so they feel comfortable sharing what they are hearing.

## RITUAL AND CEREMONY

Years before I was a change consultant, I worked at a privately-run organisation that transformed from being controlled by a team of only four trustees to a publicly listed company. One thing I remember from that significant change was the removal of the trustees' portraits from our meeting rooms to signal a new era in the company's history. This simple act of taking away the artefacts of the 'old culture' to make way for the new, resonated with me.

As humans, our innate desire for ritual and ceremony is linked to our primal need for social connection with our clan. We spend so much time with our colleagues, they are one of our important 'tribes'. As a powerful way to help people move through transition, accept new beginnings and leave the old ways behind; it's something change practitioners need to consider in their approach. Rituals and celebrations are an important way to anchor the change into the corporate culture, yet it's an approach that's underdone when we deliver organisational change.

### #changehack 18 - tap into the power of ritual and ceremony

#### New beginnings

A ritual to kick off a project helps the team come together and understand their common purpose, reminding us we are not alone on this quest and we can count on each other.

A program director told me her story about how she kicked off a large project. She invited her project team members and steering committee to a 'commitment ceremony' where they created hand prints, with paint, on a large paper wall to symbolise their membership and commitment to the project vision and team. For the duration of the project, this served as a visual reminder for all to see.

On my very first project as a change consultant, our vendors were Swedish, so many of our team members were a long way from their homeland. I developed a 'project survival kit' for each new project member as they joined the project, which included a jar of our iconic Aussie spread, Vegemite. Through the survival kit, we conveyed the message that as in most projects, there were some tough times ahead, but we could meet our challenges with cohesion and sometimes, humour...and, errrh... Vegemite!

#### Rituals for ongoing cohesion

Daily stand-up meetings and end-of-iteration retrospectives all form part of regular rituals. As social beings, we like rituals to endorse our sense of belonging and provide anchors of certainty. Something as simple as birthdays celebrated with cake and coffee on intense projects, provide light relief and bonding for the team. It's often the small, thoughtful things that are remembered and valued.

Often, you only begin to miss your old rituals when you leave to work elsewhere and adopt new practices.

### *Don't forget to celebrate the small wins!*

In the movie, The Intern, ringing the bell loudly visibly signalled an accomplishment. This reminds us to catch people doing it right to reinforce the behaviours we want to embed, during the transition and after implementation. Just like in the movie, empower all employees to publicly cheer others on with a bell or recognition wall to acknowledge good performance. What's not to like about that? It also plays to the 'progress principle' where achievement of small things keeps us motivated and engaged.

### *Endings and closure*

I heard a great example of a transition ritual on Dr Jen Frahm's short podcast with Bronte Jackson, on her *Conversations of Change* website. To introduce a new strategy and ways of working in the government sector, Bronte set up a 'transition tunnel' to farewell the old. The ritual involved acknowledging past achievements, and then walking into the tunnel with a balloon that represented the past. During the walk-through, the participants were asked to let go of, or destroy their balloon. As they came through the tunnel, they received a new balloon with the new mantra. This sent the clear message: 'we are doing things differently around here now'.

What do our people need to let go of, or receive, to adopt the new ways? If we go back to my earlier example of removing artefacts of an old culture, perhaps it's the burning or disposal of old manuals or performance scorecards? When we moved to flexi-desking, we all received a very funky pencil case and zip-up document folder to hold our stationery items and papers, to make packing up and desk-hopping easier. Post photos of your transition and closure ceremonies on your Enterprise Social Network and visual management board to continue to embed your change message.

In the natural world, recurring events such as the turning of the seasons and moon cycles are markers of new beginnings, endings and rebirth. Change in our professional and personal lives follows similar, although less predictable, cycles. Our tribal ancestors understood this and worked through the process of transition and acceptance with their rituals.

Throughout human history, social groups have benefited from the cohesion that the common experience of rituals and traditions offer. They provide a sense of tribal belonging that resonates with our innate need to connect with others and share similar experiences. Ritual and ceremony help us let go of old ways and embrace the new, in a way that engages our hearts and minds.

## THE HUMAN ELEMENT

While organisations and communities are made up of people, we can expect that our hardwired responses will underpin how we learn and respond to new information. Understanding our hardwired behaviour and responses helps us plan and deliver change in a way that resonates with our primal instincts. These insights help us get the best out of ourselves and the people we lead.

There are also numerous hardwired, cognitive biases that impact our decision making and overall behaviour, which you can explore further.

The more we know about how we are wired to behave, the more we can do to hack for change and ***make change stick!***

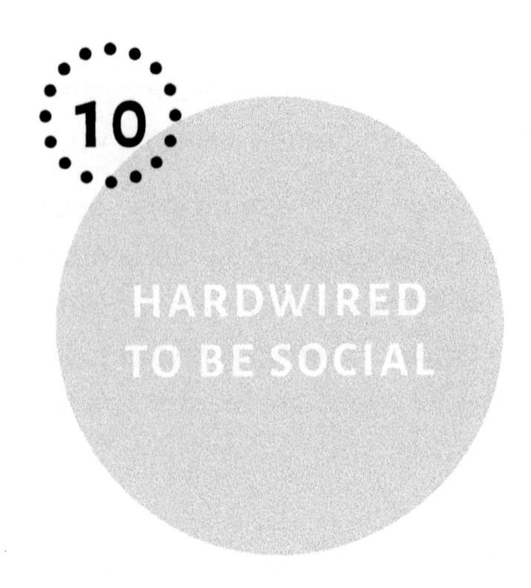


Imagine we are in France in the early 1800s. It's just after the revolution and there is great social reform. A Ministry of Education is created to oversee secular and free education. However, there is one major challenge: there is a teacher shortage. Until they can train sufficient teachers, an interim measure is introduced. They 'borrow' a method from England and call it *école mutuelle*. Translated, this means mutual school, which is peer-to-peer learning. In this environment, the students learn to read and write from older students, and generally complete a six-year curriculum in a two- to three-year period.

At their peak, more than 2,000 of these mutual schools in France, mainly in the cities, co-existed with denominational (predominantly Church) schools with traditional, hierarchical teaching in place. Success ahead of its time can be a blessing and a curse, and in this case the success of peer learning was regarded as a threat to order and respect for traditional teaching. The learning model that was born out of necessity wasn't to survive the perceived threat to conventional education and authority.

It's believed that the history and success of these schools has been deliberately suppressed to this day. In fact, most of the information available on the *école mutuelle* is still written in French. Why were these mutual schools so successful? The answer lies in the fact that we are hardwired to be social – we are instinctively social creatures. It is a human characteristic that we can tap into to help us work collaboratively through change.

We learn best from our peers. The key take-away for us is that social learning works!

## WE ARE INSTINCTIVELY SOCIAL

When we work against human instincts, we make our job a great deal harder. With recent research into brain science we are discovering insights that challenge some of our earlier theories and models on human motivation and performance. Social Neuroscientist Dr Matthew Lieberman, in his book *Social – why our brains are wired to connect*, explores this in great detail. He explains that due to our social biases and evolution, our motivation for social connection is far greater than our pursuit of self-interest. So we are wired for both competition and co-operation; however, co-operation wins. Functional MRI equipment has proven that there is increased activity in the reward centres of our brains when we collaborate.

### *Conventional thinking*

If we recall earlier thinking about human motivation, a popular model is Maslow's hierarchy of needs. Developed in the 1940s by Abraham Maslow, this famous hierarchy is typically depicted as a triangle, and represents the stages of growth through which we humans progress. The most fundamental needs are at the bottom, and only when those needs are satisfied can we be motivated to move to the next level. At the top of the pyramid, he has 'self-actualisation' – the stage when all our other basic needs are met and we can explore and realise our full potential in our chosen field.

### *Challenging convention*

In his research carried out with brain imaging technology, Lieberman has gathered insights to challenge Maslow's hierarchy of needs and offers an alternative version. His alternative view recognises that our most basic, fundamental need is for social interaction. We need human contact and interaction with others from the moment we are born.

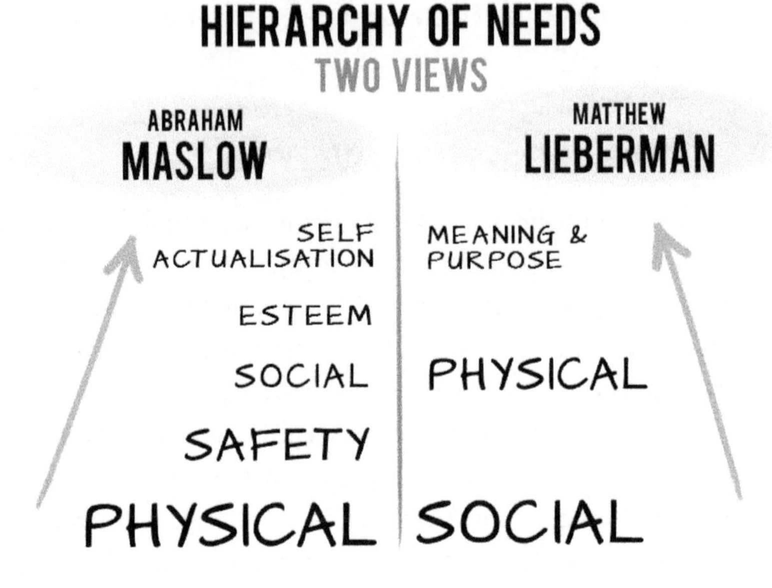


**SOURCE:** Lieberman, M. D. (2013) *Social: Why our brains are wired to connect*

### *Social rejection*

Through findings in brain science, we know that social pain, such as exclusion, activates the same neural activity as physical pain. Whether social exclusion is intentional or not, the perception alone of rejection from a group or event is enough to activate the threat response, which can be measured with fMRIs. Our sensitivity to social inclusion is so strong, any threat to it impacts our well-being.

The old proverb *'sticks and stones may break my bones, but words will never break me'*, with its many variations, had the good intention to build resilience to name-calling and other verbal taunts. But we all know how hurtful words are, as is the 'silent treatment' of exclusion. When there are signals that we don't really belong to a group, our brains process the experience as pain.

We've all heard the saying that two certainties in life are death and taxes. Well, let's add redundancy to that list. If the news of redundancy is met with surprise and sadness, this is the deepest social cut of all in a workplace context. Let's consider how this impacts the human need for social connection. In a hunting and gathering society, a way of living in which we've spent most of our human history, expulsion from the tribe or clan almost certainly meant death. Physical survival without the support and company of clan members was a challenge. Equally tough was the psychological and emotional damage caused by losing face, and not being able to return. Now, in an organisational setting, exile by redundancy is less severe for most, as the employee is likely to have a supporting network of family and friends. But we can't overlook the emotional impact of severing one channel of social connection.

When redundancies are involved, don't forget the people who stay in the organisation. They are likely to be experiencing 'survivor guilt' as they have lost members of their *workplace tribe*. While they are 'grieving' the loss of their team members, they may also feel a sense of injustice, and could be fearing the next cycle of redundancies and whether they will be impacted.

Some employees can't make sense of the changes taking place, or how decisions were made to let some people go, and are not sure how to behave or what to say to their impacted co-workers. Very few organisations acknowledge this emotion, or prepare the survivors for restructures that result in job losses. In the next chapter, on *The Truth About Resistance,* we'll see how survivor guilt can contribute to feelings of uncertainty and loss.

## HOW WE LEARN BEST

### *Social learning is on the money*

There is a mindset held by many employees that you need to attend a face-to-face formal learning program, often quite expensive, to learn.

The ***école mutuelle*** story reminds us that you don't need a big budget or formal channels to learn quickly and effectively. This may take some convincing, so one way is to tell the story about what happened in France. You may need a couple of other hacks to get the message through.

### #changehack 19 - remind people how we learn when we want to and need to

When I first introduced the concept of social and self-directed learning, I needed to provoke some thinking on the various effective ways we learn, especially when we want to know something right now. I opened with this activity, which you can try as a hack:

- ask everyone to stand up
- ask them to remain standing if they have either a Facebook account and/or a LinkedIn profile
- ask them to *remain standing* if they have paid to attend a formal training course on how to use one of those social networks
- then ask a few people who have sat down how they learned to use their networks.

My estimate is that less than 5% of your audience will remain standing as most of them will have learned by trial and error, or asked friends to show them. Welcome to social learning! Most of us are already learning socially and haven't reflected on it, or labelled it. If it works for these popular programs that are an integral part of our lives, it will work for other things you want to learn.

Be creative when thinking about your development and how to help others learn. Often, the best approach is to throw yourself into a task, project or role that you've never done before.

More recently, with the growing use and availability of social networks through the internet, there are more opportunities for self-directed learning and connection than ever before. This significantly expands the opportunities to learn through others and with others. In a later chapter, we will explore tips on how to build and develop your own Personal

Learning Network, which will be a hack for yourself. Self-directed learning is your way to acquire information when you need it, just in time and to stay ahead of the curve!

### *Social learning at its best*

Some great ideas come from building on existing ones, and that's exactly what happened when I developed and implemented a social learning mechanism, called *NED talks,* at the bank. Building on the successful formula of TED talks, NED stands for Nimble Education Delivery. NED talks provided a forum for our employees to share their expertise and connect with fellow employees by delivering a lunchtime talk of no more than 20 minutes in duration.

As a learning channel, these talks enabled our employees to tap into expertise and knowledge beyond their own teams. This low-cost initiative proved to be a successful hack in breaking down silos across the organisation while it promoted a spirit of shared learning and collaboration. The impact of the talks was enduring as we recorded each talk to make it available via our company intranet.

We ended up with a list of employees from all divisions wanting to deliver a NED talk. People were listing the activity of doing a NED talk on their professional development plans. The talks supported the organisational values of respecting and engaging our people by providing opportunities for personal and professional growth for ***both*** speakers and learners. It's a perfect example of peer teaching in action. Every way we looked at NED, it was a win/win outcome.

Shorter versions of the NED talk are *lightning talks* and *pecha cucha*, both appearing more frequently on conference agendas as our attention spans are contracting. A *lightning talk* lasts for no more than five minutes, often done *without slides*, and is an effective way for team members to report on an event they've attended. In a conference setting, slides are set to move every 15 seconds so you are disciplined to stay on topic and on time. By contrast, *pecha cucha*, the Japanese phrase for 'chit-chat', is known as the 20x20 presentation; 20 slides which are ideally images and little or no text, each shown for 20 seconds, making the duration six to seven minutes.

The good news is that there is no barrier to starting up similar sessions in any organisation and calling them any name that works for you!

We knew we were onto to a good formula with the NED talks when this initiative was recognised by the Australian Institute of Training and Development (AITD), by winning the inaugural excellence award for social and collaborative learning in 2015.

### *Key success features*

As the start-up person for NED talks, I can vouch for three key elements in our approach that helped make the program a success:

**1** | Thinking lean

**2** | Being bold – start-up mentality

**3** | Leveraging Enterprise Social Networking.

When I prepared the winning submission for the industry award, I asked our NED speakers, audience members and ambassadors for feedback and what they enjoyed, or didn't, about their NED user experience. The feedback was overwhelmingly positive. This confirmed that our value proposition was understood and they provided me with great insights into what made this initiative a success.

Here they are:

- Accessibility of the talk after the event;
- Opportunity to connect with other colleagues you may not meet in your day-to-day activity;
- Duration of the talk, and scheduling at lunchtime, was minimal intrusion to work deliverables and schedules;
- Ability to share knowledge and gain knowledge;

- Some employees established informal mentoring relationships with speakers after the talk;
- Encouraged learners to become speakers;
- Speakers found they gained a fresh perspective on their 'topic' through the questions asked and the online banter on Yammer afterwards;
- Unleashed skills and expertise within the business, which may have otherwise been 'untapped' knowledge and potential;
- Discussion of the topic with team members afterwards kept the learning alive;
- It was a safe forum for a speaker to share knowledge and gain confidence in public speaking.

### *#changehack 20 – unleash your internal talent for social learning*

Using my tips and approach for the NED talks, create a similar channel in your organisation. You can start small within your own team and grow the idea to business areas outside your team.

### *#changehack 21 – share what you learn with others*

A proven concept is teaching to learn, or 'learn by teaching' as we saw in the story about successful peer-to-peer learning in France; it is also named by scientists as the '*protégé* effect': when someone knows they will be teaching the information to others, they will make a greater effort to understand the material and learn it more thoroughly. There is the added motive to learning for yourself. It's already working with successful results in schools and universities across the United States. For example, the University of Pennsylvania has implemented a 'cascading mentoring program' where undergraduates are encouraged to teach computer science to senior high school students, who are then asked to teach what they have learned to younger students in their school. This approach can be easily applied in organisations with yet another benefit that will not meet any objections – cost efficiencies.

### *#changehack 22 – send one person to attend a course or conference with intent to share*

Some people working as permanent - as opposed to transient or contract - employees in an organisation, are still fortunate enough to attend face-to-face courses or conferences paid for by their employer. Ahhh...the memories! Next time a team member attends a formal learning event, ask them to come back and share their key learnings to the team, either as a lightning talk or *pecha cucha*, or to present a lunchtime session that is longer in duration.

### *#changehack 23 – encourage team members to run a project spotlight*

A variation of the concept of teaching to learn is to encourage team members to share their learning, outside their immediate team, after any experiment, or during or after any project. Assure them that it's okay to talk about what didn't work as well as their successes. What would they do differently next time? What advice would they give for the next group or iteration? If it's during a project or work that is still underway, position it as a spotlight session to openly talk about your project's goals and status, much like working out loud. You could kick this off by doing one yourself to lead by example and encourage this activity as regular practice.

When you are planning a learning program as part of a change initiative, consider integrating a peer-to-peer approach. Involve your change champions and other users as peer coaches, so the learning content itself is co-created. While they are creating the learning program, with the intent to coach and teach others, their own learning is invaluable.

So if you want to learn lots with little financial outlay, then the answer lies in how we are hardwired to connect and learn. It seems so straightforward, yet under-utilised. Often the knowledge and expertise we need is right in front of us – but we have never asked or looked. Open up the channels and you will be pleasantly surprised with what you discover and who you meet!

# 11 THE TRUTH ABOUT RESISTANCE

As we've seen in the last two chapters, understanding our hardwired behaviour and responses helps us plan and deliver change in a way that resonates with our primal instincts. It helps us understand how it impacts human performance and how we can get the best out of ourselves and the **people** we lead.

The more we know about how we are hardwired to respond, the more we can do to hack for change and ***make change stick.***

We also have brain science on our side, as we are finding out more about our primal behaviour that helps us understand the human response to change itself.

Do we really naturally resist change? Now that neuroscience is converging with behavioural science, we have new insights into how our brain processes change and filters new information. With these new insights, it's time to re-think our assumptions that people will naturally resist change. Our change plans and interventions usually assume resistance, when in fact the human response can be either to resist or to support. The key is to find out why the response to the same change can trigger a range of varied experiences and emotional responses.

## THE HUMAN PARADOX

As humans, we are wired to resist change in some instances, yet embrace it at other times. This may sound confusing; however, if we wholeheartedly disliked change, how could we be the most adaptable species on the planet? Why did we bother to venture out of the trees, roam the savannah, walk upright, diversify our diet, and eventually manipulate many aspects of our natural environment? Yet we resist the introduction of a new system or structure at work.

We can find the answers and deeper insights through the relatively new discipline of neuroscience. As 90% of what we know about the brain has only been discovered in the last ten or so years, brain scanning technology is now shedding light onto this human paradox – not only ***why*** it exists, but also ***when*** and ***how*** exposure to new stimuli registers as discomfort in the brain. What does this now mean for change practitioners and leading others through transformation?

## CHANGE IS NOW AN ART AND A SCIENCE

Until very recently, change management as a discipline fell neatly into the category of social science. Social science traditionally explores the human mind and behaviour through observation and conclusion, whereas neuroscience studies the anatomy and physiology of the brain and can observe responses with imaging technology. Before we delve into the workings of our primal brain, let's take a closer look at what the field of neuroscience is revealing.

Neuroscientist Dr David Rock, a key Australian researcher in this emerging field, has helped bring together the disciplines of neuroscience and behavioural science and coined the term *'NeuroLeadership',* which is made up of these four domains:

**1** | Decision making and problem solving

**2** | Emotional regulation

3 | Collaboration and influence

4 | Change leadership.

Using brain-based research and imaging technology, David Rock, along with other neuroscientists, has compiled scientific data to complement earlier behavioural studies. Simply put, they've added a hard edge to what is often considered a soft science, whilst providing new insights into effective leadership and inspiring employee engagement.

## IS IT RESISTANCE OR A RESPONSE?

As humans, we are hardwired to minimise threat and maximise reward. David Rock developed the SCARF model for looking at the primal reaction in the human brain to situations of threat or reward, which can now be measured by imaging technology such as functional Magnetic Resonance Imaging (fMRI). Understanding our neural responses makes perfect sense. The physiology of our brain hasn't changed in 200,000 years, so it's no surprise that our responses will be our hardwired and instinctive.

### *Our response to loss*

There's the gambler who chases his losses; or the project managers who are reluctant to shut down their program of work due to 'sunk costs'. Our built-in aversion to loss drives us to make poor decisions that defy logic. Despite how rational we are most of the time, our emotion relating to loss has primal roots. It is so strong that it overrides our opportunity to gain. When there is uncertainty, our brains register this experience of 'not knowing' as a loss. When we experience a sense of loss, we feel threatened. Feeling overwhelmed by threat means our ability to make decisions, solve problems and communicate is impaired.

Our response to loss is elegantly expressed in David Rock's SCARF model of threat and reward. When one of the elements in the SCARF model is reduced or taken away, our brain activates a threat response. If an element is increased or granted to us, we activate a reward response. SCARF stands for:

S – Status

C – Certainty

A - Autonomy

R - Relatedness

F – Fairness

Here's a brief overview of the SCARF model and how it relates to our responses to change and new information.

### *Status*

We have a hard-wired social need for respect, esteem and a place in a 'pecking order'. A perception of one's status being lowered will trigger the threat response, which is similar to a primal threat to one's safety. When our status is threatened, we may defend a position that we don't agree with, simply to avoid the perceived pain associated with a drop in status.

### *Certainty*

We like to know what will happen next. When an unfamiliar or new situation is presented, the brain is confused and works overtime to make sense of the situation, taking up more neural energy. When uncertainty increases, memory and commitment decline. This validates many existing change models that acknowledge a period of lower productivity during times of transformation.

### *Autonomy*

The opportunity to make choices or to exercise some control over one's environment also increases the sense of certainty, therefore reducing stress. Allowing people to make autonomous decisions increases motivation and engagement, whilst a leader who micro-manages will have the opposite effect. Even the perception of autonomy is important.

### *Relatedness*

We need to feel safe around people in our group/s. Social connection is a primal need. The brain is programmed to classify a person as 'friend' or 'foe'. A 'foe' triggers a threat response. Interestingly, social neuroscientists have found that social exclusion creates the same neural response as physical pain. This means social pain is like physical pain.

### *Fairness*

An experience of unfairness, even if only a perception, will result in less productivity and more negativity, registering the same brain response as physical pain. Fairness is perceived in relative terms. For example, even if not motivated by financial rewards, people will regard the situation as unfair if they feel they are underpaid relative to their peers. Yet a perceived improvement in fairness activates the same neural response as receiving a monetary reward or eating chocolate.

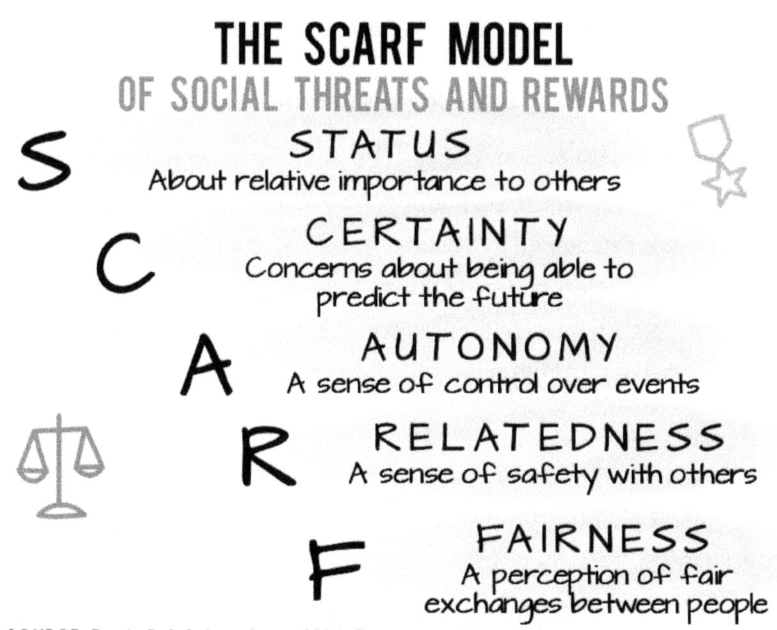


**SOURCE:** Rock. D & Schwartz, J. (2006) *The neuroscience of leadership*

## WHAT LEADERS CAN DO

Here's the catch for leaders when there is change or disruption - the threat response, ie the response to any perceived loss, is stronger, lasts longer and occurs faster. The default human response is to avoid the loss or run away from the threat ***before*** we move towards a reward.

But there is good news. By understanding the implications of the SCARF model, leaders can motivate employees with non-financial rewards. When Mark Twain said *'I can live for a month on a good compliment',* he already knew that it's not just monetary incentives that activate our reward circuitry in the brain.

fRMI scanning reveals that change does 'hurt' when it is experienced as a threat, making the pain associated with transformation a reality. When a change or new information is perceived as a gain, the reward circuitry in the brain is activated. So both resistance (loss) and reward (gain) have a neurological basis.

The key message for leaders is to minimise the threat response for optimal performance and improved employee engagement.

### ***#changehack 24 – run a team self-assessment session***

Keep in mind that we vary in our responses or perception to each element in the SCARF model. One team member may feel strongly about relatedness, while another is threatened by a change in status. In all elements, perception is as powerful as reality, and perception alone can provoke a threat response. SCARF elements are inter-related, as one event can trigger emotion in more than one area. For example, a drop in status can be regarded as unfair.

Models like the SCARF framework are great in theory. The hack is to use this model to find out how your team is feeling, as individuals and collectively. This will promote open discussion about the sentiment, and uncover where the 'pain points' and 'reward points' are for your team.

I often facilitate this session for teams about to experience change, particularly organisational change. After a brief introduction to Rock's SCARF model, and how change is new normal these days, we typically brainstorm and discuss how the team members felt themselves to be impacted by each SCARF element.

| Emotional Driver | To what extent are these questions being addressed? |
|---|---|
| **S**tatus<br>About relative importance to others. | Will I be seen as competent in this transformation/ change?<br>How will my capability be seen by others? By my new leader?<br>Does the change negatively impact on my sense of status? My employees' status? |
| **C**ertainty<br>Concerns being able to predict the future. | Do I know what the future holds for me?<br>What level of certainty is there for my team?<br>Does the change provide certainty regarding timelines, outcomes? |
| **A**utonomy<br>Provides a sense of control over events. | Do I have control and any choice in this change?<br>Do employees have enough autonomy to complete their work, and decide how they will work through the change?<br>To what extent has my level of autonomy changed? My team members' autonomy?<br>Have I given too much autonomy? |
| **R**elatedness<br>A sense of safety with others, of friend or foe. | Do I feel connected to anyone or isolated in this change?<br>Does the change negatively impact how employees interact with one another?<br>To what degree have teams shifted, regrouped, acquired new leaders, or 'lost' team members to restructures? Is there a sentiment of 'survivor guilt'? |
| **F**airness<br>A perception of fair exchanges between people. | Am I being treated fairly in this transformation or change?<br>Will the change/transformation be perceived as fair by my team?<br>How do I recognise good effort? Do I do this fairly across my team/s? |

*Source: My white paper on the neuroscience of change, found on my website, titled: 'Navigating through transformation: A neuroscience-based toolkit for change', 2014*

Then I hand out the self-assessment template below (which I developed), and ask each person to evaluate how they experienced, as an individual, the scale of emotion for each SCARF element. This process allows each team member to reflect on their response, as they plot it on the threat/reward scale on the template.

We then collate each team member's rating on a flipchart sheet to see a picture of the extent of the team's pain points by each SCARF element. This helps them to label their feelings through awareness and drives a productive discussion on how they will manage the challenges ahead as a group. It also helps the team leader understand how their team is feeling, which provides valuable clues for further coaching conversations and support to reduce the threat response.

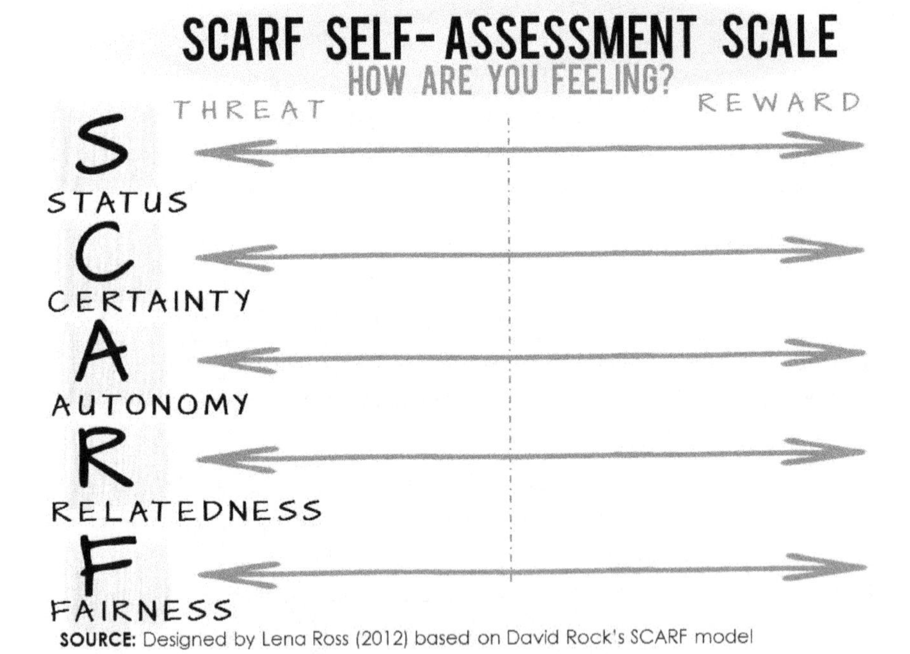


**SOURCE:** Designed by Lena Ross (2012) based on David Rock's SCARF model

### *#changehack 25 – gather tips to reduce the threat response*

Brainstorm tips on how to reduce the threat response with your leadership teams; to build on it, add your own ideas to make it relevant to your workplace culture and change scenario.

To get you started, here are some examples on what you can do:

| Emotional Driver | What leaders can do |
|---|---|
| **S**tatus<br>About relative importance to others. | • Acknowledge subject matter expertise and seek it out, no matter where they stand in the 'pecking order'.<br>• Lead by example, practise what you preach. Don't use positional power to exempt yourself from what you expect others to do.<br>• If a team member's status has been reduced, find another way to reward them that gives them status in the group. |
| **C**ertainty<br>Concerns being able to predict the future. | • If you can't communicate details, do communicate ***when*** further details will be available. Providing a date provides a small anchor of certainty.<br>• Plug into the grapevine or carry out pulse checks to uncover what may be causing anxiety.<br>• Discuss rumours openly. Provide a forum for rumour busting. |
| **A**utonomy<br>Provides a sense of control over events. | • Start performance feedback conversations with the question - how do you think you are going?<br>• Explore every opportunity to co-create an approach to the change, eg Lean Coffee, forums, workshops, working out loud. |
| **R**elatedness<br>A sense of safety with others, of friend or foe. | • The sense of belonging to a group is critical. Look for opportunities to introduce or encourage your people to participate in buddy systems, mentoring, reverse-mentoring and change networks.<br>• Let people know you've 'got their back' and you are prepared to support them.<br>• Support informal collaboration channels, such as Enterprise Social Networks/Yammer, to build a sense of 'community'. |

| | |
|---|---|
| **F**airness<br>A perception of fair exchanges between people. | • Be clear and transparent about how and why decisions will be made.<br>• Keep private and sensitive conversations private - especially as most of us now work in open-plan work spaces.<br>• Understand and acknowledge 'survivor guilt' when the change involves organisational restructure. When team members leave, those left behind are left wondering. This is also an emotional driver for relatedness. |

*Source: My white paper on the neuroscience of change, found on my website, titled: 'Navigating through transformation: A neuroscience-based toolkit for change', 2014*

The good news is that there are multiple applications of this knowledge, particularly for leaders:

- self-awareness
- team/group awareness
- coaching
- framing communication
- leading teams
- engaging with stakeholders
- curating a library of actions.

Along with the benefits of understanding our team's response to change and new information, understanding our own primal response is a valuable way to improve our self-awareness. It helps us understand why we can get fired up so easily, and what we can do about it.

*A key benefit of understanding our hardwired responses and running workshops with our impacted employees to understand what triggers threat, is that it provides a forum for people to talk about how they are feeling and what they are thinking.*

*It legitimises a conversation about emotions that may otherwise not occur.*

### *There are business benefits too!*

Minimising threat means a more engaged workforce. And we know engaged workers are more productive and less resistant to change, so business benefits can be realised faster from transformation efforts. The more informed we are about what is happening at an emotional level, the better we can 'unpack' the nature of the threat response, and 'hack' the potential loss in productivity. We can minimise that dip that often happens.

THE PRODUCTIVITY DIP

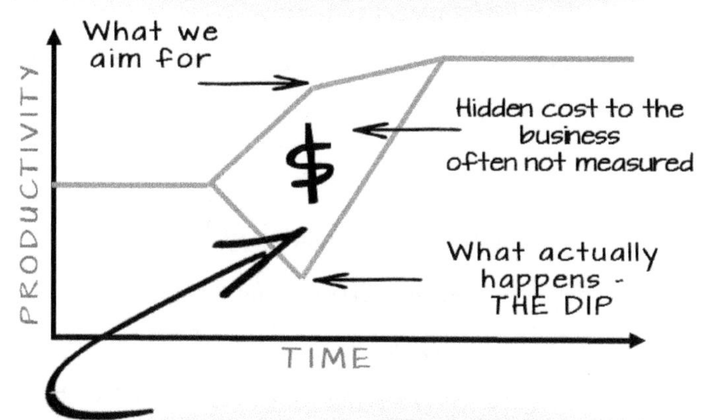


WITH OUR NEW INSIGHTS FROM BRAIN SCIENCE, WE CAN UNPACK WHAT'S GOING ON IN HERE TO UNDERSTAND WHAT PEOPLE ARE EXPERIENCING

**SOURCE:** Inspired by various change curves that feature the *Valley of Despair*

With technology and other global forces demanding unprecedented agility to remain competitive, neuroscience offers organisations a clear value proposition. As long as humans continue to work in organisations, human performance and employee engagement will be integral to business performance. With ways of scientifically monitoring human behaviour, the application of findings from neuroscience can only improve business success. An engaged workforce means less resistance so business benefits can be realised faster from transformation efforts.

Now that we can observe and measure neural activity in response to specific actions and behaviours, we can confidently re-position the 'soft science' of change management as hard.

For leaders and change practitioners, a better understanding of our brain function helps us improve performance at individual, team and enterprise levels to enable more successful change. We can rethink some of our existing practices and look at the human response through the 'neuro-lens' to improve engagement and productivity. You could say neuroscience is 'on the money'!

With SCARF as a framework for understanding our response to change and new information, we can consider our primal reactions and behaviours in all our change hacks for stakeholder engagement, collaborative learning and communication.

---

*Organisations are made up of* ***PEOPLE***

*Threat comes at a* ***COST*** *to the organisation*

***REDUCE*** *the threat*

*Optimise the* ***PERFORMANCE*** *and*
***MOTIVATION*** *of your* ***PEOPLE***

---

# WHAT YOU DO & DELIVER

AGILE AS A CAPABILITY
What you
DO & DELIVER
How you
ACT
How you
THINK
PRACTICES
BEHAVIOURS
MINDSET
ORGANISATIONAL
AGILITY
© Lena Ross, 2016

# 12 AGILE PRACTICES

In many organisations, we're seeing a shift to an increasingly Agile project environment, sometimes alongside an operating environment that is defined as agile. Within that broad definition of agile comes a range of practices that can be applied to a project that is not strictly defined as 'Agile'. It's becoming increasingly common to hear of change practitioners working on what they define as a 'hybrid' project, where a conventional waterfall project is starting to adopt agile practices. You may hear the 'hybrid' approach also called 'wagile' to represent the blend of the two words 'waterfall' and 'agile'. While this may not sit too well with agile purists, it's happening nonetheless.

So it's out there. The hybrid project means that change professionals are expected to adopt agile practices, often with very little guidance or confidence. Whilst there isn't a formula or roadmap on how to apply agile change practices in your hybrid project, a few change hacks are useful to get started. With agile - sometimes referred to as 'lean' - as an underpinning principle, some of these hacks may appear to be slightly disruptive and confronting, rapid and iterative, but overall they carry the honourable intent of engagement and involvement.

If your change initiative happens to be following a clearly defined Agile approach, then these practices still apply to you.

Now the rubber can really hit the ground!

Agile practices can be applied in all your change planning and your day-to-day engagement with project team members, stakeholders and end users. The practices will promote deeper engagement and co-creation with your stakeholders.

## NOW, LET'S DO IT

Here's a list of the practices covered in this chapter:

- Stand-up meeting
- Change canvas
- Kanban board
- Lean coffee
- Working out loud with
  - Showcases
  - Think tanks
- Gamification
- Retrospective
- Future-spective.

In the chapters that follow, we will look at how to build and tell your story, identifying and prioritising your stakeholders, and some facilitation hacks to promote collaboration and deeper engagement.

### *Stand-up meeting*

One of the most visible agile practices is the team stand-up meeting. Treated like a ritual, this is sometimes referred to as a daily scrum meeting. By being short and frequent, these meetings help teams develop the desired behaviours by becoming more productive and transparent in their work. For many, this practice alone requires a shift in behaviour and mindset.

The best place for the daily stand-up is in front of your visual management board where the progress of the team's work is visible. They shouldn't take longer than 15 minutes at the start of each work day. Each team member addresses these three questions:

- What I did since the last meeting
- What I will do until the next meeting
- What's getting in my way.

It's worth noting that the daily stand-up meeting doesn't replace planning meetings or other catch-up sessions between the scrum master and team members that need to take place.

### *Change canvas*

In the spirit of lean and visual management, the change canvas is a brilliant one-page view of the change plan. It usually includes the case for the change and provides early insights into the scope of the initiative, helping build rationale for dedicated change management resources.

The poster-size version of the change canvas is the highly visible one to post on the project's visual management board. Start adding information in discussions with your project team members and product owner (sponsor). In a non-agile project, you can glean a great deal of information from the project plan or business case to build your change canvas. Leave open space on your canvas to invite comments and questions on post-it notes.

The change canvas is one of the documents that I carry around with me (in A3 size) to drive and support my change conversations. Here's an example of one I've used that can be adapted to your initiative.

THE CHANGE CANVAS
AN EXAMPLE

PRODUCT OWNER ............ CHANGE LEAD ............
Change being introduced ............ Date ............
Problem (the WHAT) Solution (the HOW) Value Proposition (the WHY)
Customers/stakeholders (WHO) Time & effort needed
- COMMUNICATION -
Existing channels Key messages - W I F M
Success criteria Risks & issues (high level)


### *The Kanban board*

What a great word - *Kanban*. It's the Japanese word for visual signal or card.

Inspired by the lean manufacturing practices at Toyota, the Kanban board is an effective, visual way for agile teams (and any other teams) to display what they are doing and where it's at. Combine it with the stand-up meeting and you have a visual tool at hand to discuss the progress of your work.

One of the objectives of Kanban is to bring attention to the volume of work in process - in the 'doing' column - in order to reduce it. The idea is to move work along the flow, to the 'done' column.

At a glance, you see not only the progress, but also the scope and scale of work underway. You can make it more meaningful by colour coding post-it notes, or adding *avatars*, for each team member. For the uninitiated, an avatar is a graphic, cartoon-like representation of a real team member. An avatar adds a fun, colourful element to the visual management board too.

***Lean Coffee***

A discussion about agile or lean change is not complete without a commentary on the concept of Lean Coffee. It claims its roots back in 2009, when a couple of agile thought leaders wanted to start a group of like-minded people to discuss Lean techniques to meet informally, in the spirit of collaborative learning. And so the concept of Lean Coffee was born - and took off.

It's a democratic meeting with some structure and no agenda. Participants gather and decide on the agenda together. With lean principles in mind, the structure is minimal. Here's how it works:

1 | Schedule a meeting. Pique interest by calling it Lean Coffee.

2 | Be sure to take post-it notes and have a wall or flipchart stand handy.

**3** | Set up a different version of a Kanban board to show the progress of the meeting, with these three suggested headings: *to discuss, discussing* and *discussed.*

**4** | People write on post-it notes the topics they want to discuss, and place them in the 'to discuss' column. Encourage as many ideas possible.

**5** | Allow each person to introduce their topic in one or two sentences.

**6** | Each participant get two votes. You can vote twice for the same thing, or one vote per topic, by placing a dot or tick next to the one you support.

**LEAN COFFEE**

**EXAMPLE OF OPEN INVITATION**

Join us for LEAN COFFEE

LEAN COFFEE is an informal session where we will discuss the new **change framework and approach.**

It will be a structured session where you determine the agenda.

WHERE?
Level 8 open
café area

CONTACT?
Lena Ross
<email address>

WHEN?
Monday 15 March
10.00am

No RSVP needed
Just rock up!

WHAT to BRING
An open mind!

### *Benefits*

- Replaces the rigours of a formal working group. If you can't escape the formal working group, it provides an additional engagement channel.

- Helps you identify your early adopters and supporters, who are your potential change champions.
- Uncovers pockets of resistance and why there is potential threat.
- Provides insights into the topics and issues that are top of mind.
- You will have an inside view on the 'word on the street' or any gossip and misunderstandings about the change.
- Addresses our primal need for *autonomy*, providing a low-threat, informal place for discussion where the participants drive the agenda.

### *Working out loud practices*

Working out loud was mentioned in an earlier chapter, as one of the three communication channels that promote co-creation and collaboration. By working out loud we carry out our work in a way that is highly visible to our peers and stakeholders. This practice is consistent with the agile team values of transparency and openness about your work. Running a *showcase session* or hosting a *think tank* are two ways to work out loud that invite engagement and conversation.

### *Showcase session*

A showcase is a scheduled session. or a series of sessions. for stakeholders and other employees in your organisation who may be interested in your change initiative. As the word suggests, it's a great way to 'showcase' your project and the benefits it will deliver.

Schedule your session in a way that invites audience participation. This can be as simple as a quiz, where the answers are provided along the way, with quirky prizes. Or you can keep the energy levels high by breaking up the larger group into smaller ones to rotate team members, who explain or demonstrate a specific part of their work.

Assign your project a hashtag. Keep the interest alive during and after these sessions by asking people to post their key take-aways and photos on your organisation's enterprise social platform - like Yammer, remember? The Enterprise Social Network is the place for questions and answers before, during and after your event. With the hashtag, participants and team members can easily search and find relevant posts.

### Think tank

I often call my think tanks *'think-ubators'* to send a message that thinking is evolving. The think-ubator can be a permanent room or work area where the project team resides, or an assigned area close to the project team.

The think-ubator, or think tank, is a highly visual, often colourful place that attracts people. It's a place for your visitors to drop in, with opportunities for them to add thoughts with post-it notes, and ask questions. You can design it to be open at any time, or a place that has designated drop-in times. As the word itself suggests, this dedicated space is created to provoke thinking and an exchange of ideas, as well as a channel for you and your team to demonstrate what you're working on.

This space is the ideal place to display your large journey maps as well.

### #changehack 26 - host a think-ubator

A think-ubator that worked well for me was a period of post-workshop review, where I wanted to continue engagement. It looked like this:

At a workshop with my stakeholders we mapped on a very large poster-sized journey map a desired state of how our users would think and feel and what they would be doing. After the workshop, I pinned the poster in an incubator-friendly workspace where our stakeholders and end users could visit and continue to add their thoughts, with post-it notes, on the map.

We uncovered a great deal more insights by providing this forum, as people had the time to go away and reflect. As a think-ubator, this wall was a mural that our people could see, revisit and add their comments.

This holistic view resonated at many levels - it was big picture and visual. And each time they visited, it opened conversation on the big questions, such as:

- How might we make this happen?
- How can your leader help?
- How can you help?
- How can I help?

### *Gamify*

Have you ever played Candy Crush or Angry Birds? And are you addicted? Chances are that you have been 'gamified'. Gamification is the word used to describe the application of game-based principles in a non-traditional game environment, such as in an organisation.

Unfortunately, when it comes to a motivation to learn, we are not all created equal. For organisations, gamification is hailed as a way to promote and optimise engagement and learning, making it fun and motivating. Some people argue that an early form of gamification was when airlines introduced frequent flyer programs, adding a new dimension to customer loyalty by making point collection a game. Even if we don't play Candy Crush, most of us have loyalty cards from our favourite coffee shops to count down to our next free caffeine fix.

### *#changehack 27 - get onto gamification*

There's a number of ways you can gamify your learning and engagement, ranging from very simple activities to more sophisticated online versions. Some games introduce a longer-term focus with point or badge collection, real-time leader boards and avatars. If you have the luxury of budget and time, it's well worth exploring the development of software to host game-based learning.

In the meantime, you can easily integrate some games into your learning programs. Here's one I've used many times, as it can be easily tailored to different sessions.

### *The curiosity challenge*

Like an old-fashioned car rally, the goal is to find things. This time the items that collect points are pieces of information or knowledge that our impacted user needs to help them through the change. This can be knowledge about websites, intranet resources, help lines, names of key people, and other support resources.

The game rules that typically apply to all team challenges are:

- First team to complete all activities wins
- Give your team a name
- Only one laptop to be used per team during activity
- No mobile phones to be used.

### *Retrospective*

True to its definition, a 'retrospective' is about looking back. It served our species well in our hunting and gathering days when we told stories around the campfires of what worked, what didn't work, what presented danger and what provided safety. It was essential to our survival.

Ben Linders, an agile coach with a fabulous website of resources, provides this definition:

> *An agile retrospective is a practice used by teams to* ***reflect on their way of working*** *and to* ***continuously become better*** *at what they do.*

Whilst not as critical for human survival today, the practice of a retrospective continues to provide great value. In an organisational context, a retrospective needs a facilitator who can help the group review their experiment or event to discover what went well and what they can learn from the experience to improve it for next time.

### *#changehack 28 - run a retrospective*

As often as you need to, facilitate a retrospective - often called a *retro* - for your project team, and focus on three key questions:

- What went well? Capture it so you don't forget it for next time. The good lessons are just as important as what we need to improve.
- What can be improved?
- What could/should we do differently next time?

Set up a flipchart like this one and provide an abundance of post-it notes so participants can contribute freely and anonymously.

Compare this to a Post Implementation Review (PIR), which is usually facilitated at the conclusion of the entire project to review numerous aspects of the initiative. In a project that's defined as 'agile', the Retrospective is held at the end of each sprint or iteration, typically facilitated by the scrum master, so the learnings can be applied in the next sprint. On hybrid or waterfall projects, you can run a retro as often as you need to, as a shorter session, to focus on a particular aspect, such as, *how did that session go for stakeholders?*

***Retro tips***

- Set the scene that it's a safe environment to reflect
- Allow everyone to have a voice
- Agree on next steps
- Assign actions and owners
- Make it no longer than 60 minutes
- Take a photo of your retro flipchart
- Make your learnings visible to your stakeholders, considering Yammer and visual management.

### The Future-spective

A concept devised by Ben Linders, the *future-spective* is a twist on the retrospective. The future-paced version of the retrospective is carried out at the beginning of a project to help teams plan their approach.

By visualising they are at the conclusion of the sprint and have achieved their goal, agile team members discuss:

- What does it look like, this end of iteration state?
- What helped us get there?
- What got in the way? What didn't work or made it hard for us to reach our goals? What unexpected events could derail the change effort?

When team members imagine what could fail or present a challenge, they prepare themselves for many scenarios and anticipate creative solutions.

### #changehack 29 - run a future-spective for your team

Based on Ben Linders' definition of a future-spective, I've designed this template to gather thoughts in a workshop:

THE FUTURE-SPECTIVE

IMAGINE WE HAVE REACHED OUR GOAL

What does it look like?

What helped?

What got in the way?

**SOURCE:** Design based on blog content on www.benlinders.com

Now that we've explored some of the key agile practices that involve change leaders and practitioners, we can see how they rely on an agile mindset and the agile behaviours of transparency and trust.

Our primal brains love stories. Before humans could read or write, we told stories orally to keep our traditions and myths alive and enduring from generation to generation. Through evolution, our brains became wired to tell and listen to stories. It was our key communication channel.

In 2012, Metro Trains (the suburban railway system in Melbourne, Australia) needed a customer awareness campaign to get a message out to its commuters to travel safely on its trains, in order to reduce the number of serious and fatal accidents that are largely preventable. If you've lived in Melbourne over the last couple of years, you will be familiar with the campaign. For the non-Melburnians among us, Metro Trains' video campaign was titled ***Dumb Ways to Die.*** It comprised a catchy tune, cute animated characters and offbeat humour.

In a nutshell, ***Dumb Ways to Die*** is contemporary storytelling. The clip tells the story of silly ways you can lose your life, including behaving irresponsibly around and on trains. Not only was it quirky, it was incredibly successful. The animated message became the most awarded campaign in the history of Cannes. At the time of writing this piece, the YouTube clip alone has had over 145 million hits!

A story with a beginning, middle and end primes the brain for an outcome and builds anticipation and interest. It evokes images, and when told effectively, it will do these three things:

**1** | It will *resonate* with people

**2** | It will be *remembered*

**3** | It will be *retold.*

It connects *the why* (the cause) with ***the what*** and ***the how*** (outcome, effect).

Hey - isn't that what we want when we deliver change? We want it to resonate, be remembered and retold.

So this makes building and telling the story of your change initiative a capability well worth developing. *You want more people engaging with their hearts and minds, while remembering and retelling the purpose and benefit of your change.* Once you master the basics, through a proven formula/ approach, you are on your way to better engagement.

## TAPPING INTO OUR NATURAL CURIOSITY

Thanks to recent findings in neuroscience, we know that our brains are more responsive to stories than a list of facts, figures or data. For example, we now know that when we read or listen to data, the language centre of our brain is activated. But when we read or hear a story, the language centre of our brain lights up along with the parts of our brain that respond when we are actually experiencing the event. Storytelling releases dopamine in our brains, which is the chemical that supports memory and accuracy.

The natural curiosity aroused by a story hooks us into wanting to hear what happens next and the final outcome. This is what makes it easier for us to remember the story. So when we talk about engaging the hearts *and* minds of our people, we need to consider the positive impact of stories on our brains.

A story establishes a connection between the story-teller and the listeners, who resonate with the words. In his TED talk in February 2016, neuroscientist Uri Hasson shared further interesting, recent findings. Using functional magnetic resonance imaging (fRMI) technology, he was able to demonstrate that when more than one participant listens to the *same* story, their brain activity becomes synched. The same alignment occurred when the same story was told in two different languages to the respective native speakers. This means that once a group hears the same story, they are very likely to align and be on the same page.

These insights further support the rationale for using story-telling techniques to build stronger relationships, which in turn improves engagement. In times when we are overwhelmed with information and data, when our attention spans appear to be shorter, there is great competition for our stakeholders' attention.

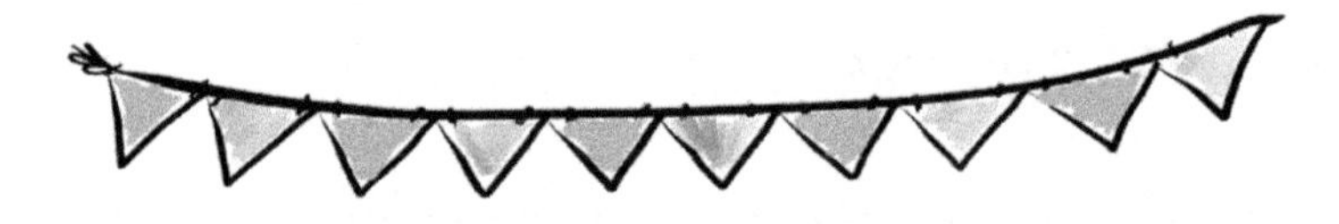

> Personal stories and gossip make up 65% of our conversations.
>
> Jeremy Hsu

You will come across numerous ways to build your story. Perhaps you've attended a storytelling workshop and picked up tips for practising your art. Many people I've worked with swear by the Pixar storytelling format, which provides a valuable framework to work with. Pixar, as most of you will know, is the animation company now owned by Disney.

In 2011 one of their former employees, Emma Coats, a story artist, started sharing her tips on storytelling, making a useful guide for screenwriters. Since then, her tweets and tips morphed into 22 story rules, which were then simplified into six steps. Phew, thankfully only six! Because we know the brain works best with ***5 plus or minus two*** pieces of information.

## THE PIXAR FORMULA

Here's the six-step Pixar formula that you can use as a framework to build your project or organisational story.

**1** | Once upon a time there was...

**2** | Every day...

**3** | Then one day...

**4** | And because of that...

**5** | And because of that...

**6** | Until finally...

### *A real example*

Here's an example of a change that's taking place in many organisations, including the 'bank', and how we told the story:

| Step | Theme | Story |
|---|---|---|
| 1 | Once there was | Just prior to the organisational realignment, there were several separate change teams in our business. These change teams were working largely independently of one another, developing their own methods and approaches, using their own frameworks to define capabilities for performance management, role assignment and recruitment. They each defined their value proposition to their project and business clients in their own way. |

| | | |
|---|---|---|
| **2** | Every day | Every now and again, the change practitioners came together as an informal community of practice to share experiences and resources. While they were collaborating informally, there was no consistent approach to the way change was defined, managed and delivered across the organisation. |
| **3** | Then one day | In 2013, the CEO announced a major organisational transformation. The key objective of the realignment was to identify areas where work effort and capabilities were duplicated so they could centralise for operational efficiencies. A new business operating model was developed to reflect the new structure and which capabilities would be centralised. Change management was one area that was impacted, as plans were underway to establish one change practice. |
| **4** | Because of that | Because of that, the newly established change practice needed to carry out a careful review of the existing, disparate approaches. It introduced a consistent methodology that was scalable and could be applied across the business to different types of change and transformation. The new methodology meant that all initiators of change, not just dedicated change practitioners, were training on the new approach, tools and templates. A capability model was also established to define what change practitioners deliver, providing a clear career path and insights into what skill set is required when recruiting. |
| **5** | And because of that | An intranet site was set up to provide a central repository of information that accommodated the documents and templates, making it easy for end users to find. A governance forum was established to provide general oversight and to gather user feedback, to ensure continued relevance, improvement and best practice. |

| | | |
|---|---|---|
| **6** | Until finally | Now, two years on, the central change practice has introduced a consistent set of approaches, tools and templates that are widely used across the enterprise. A common language is used among change practitioners and change initiators. The change practice capability framework means that project managers and other internal stakeholders have a common understanding of what dedicated change practitioners can deliver. As well as providing a consistent set of deliverables for stakeholders, the quality of documentation and knowledge management has improved. Being able to find templates, definitions and completed examples on a central online repository saves time for our internal clients. |

You can use a sheet that looks like this one. Then you can grab the key points and display them as a visual storyboard, as well as talking points for engagement sessions:

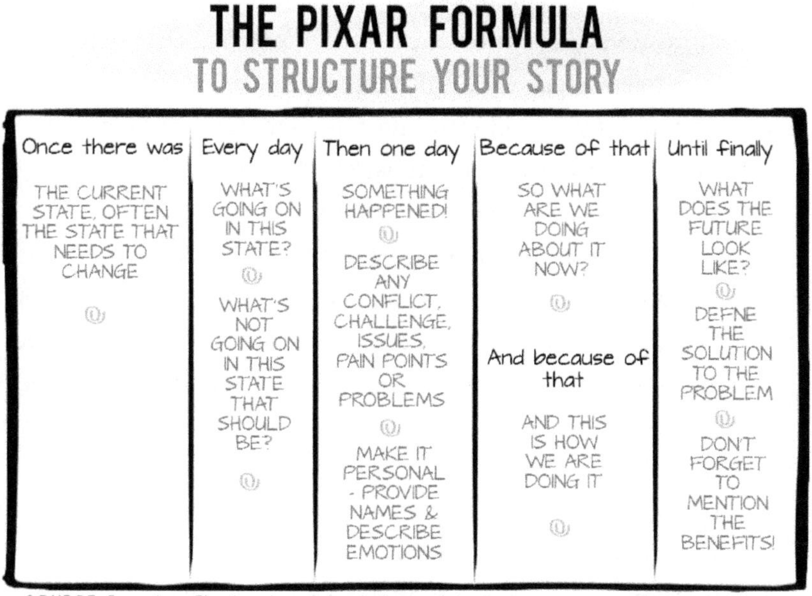

## THE PIXAR FORMULA
### TO STRUCTURE YOUR STORY

| Once there was | Every day | Then one day | Because of that | Until finally |
|---|---|---|---|---|
| THE CURRENT STATE. OFTEN THE STATE THAT NEEDS TO CHANGE | WHAT'S GOING ON IN THIS STATE? WHAT'S NOT GOING ON IN THIS STATE THAT SHOULD BE? | SOMETHING HAPPENED! DESCRIBE ANY CONFLICT, CHALLENGE, ISSUES, PAIN POINTS OR PROBLEMS. MAKE IT PERSONAL - PROVIDE NAMES & DESCRIBE EMOTIONS | SO WHAT ARE WE DOING ABOUT IT NOW? **And because of that** AND THIS IS HOW WE ARE DOING IT | WHAT DOES THE FUTURE LOOK LIKE? DEFINE THE SOLUTION TO THE PROBLEM. DON'T FORGET TO MENTION THE BENEFITS! |

**SOURCE:** Based on Pixar's rules of storytelling, originally formulated by Emma Coats

### *Making it work*

#### *#changehack 30 – help your project team build the story*

More people in your team are likely to re-tell the story if they can play a part in building it.

Run a session with your project leadership team to create the story. Here's a suggested approach you can take:

- Explain the benefits of the story telling approach (why we are doing this).
- Walk through the Pixar six-step approach as a framework (how we are doing this).
- If you have an example to show them, use that to demonstrate a complete story. It doesn't have to be work-related; you could use a Pixar example to reiterate the six steps.
- Work through one step at a time. Use butcher's paper pinned up around the room, one sheet for each step. Ask participants to write their ideas on post-it notes. As the facilitator, read out the suggestions and cluster the contributions that convey the same message. You can wordsmith this later.
- When the five or six steps are complete, arrange them in order around the room and play it back to the audience to check that it makes sense as an end-to-end story.
- Allow some white space in your agenda for discussion. These sessions often open discussions as team members need to brainstorm a little to agree on a few points. For some team members, the process itself will be invaluable clarification of the project's purpose, in plain language, and the role they will play in delivering the benefits.
- Ask for one or two volunteers to help you word-smith this story for review by the project team.
- Agree on next steps and time frames. When will the first draft be ready for review? When will the review be complete?

- Discuss how you will use the final product. How will you tell the story to stakeholders? Will you have it represented visually on a poster, or in the form of a short clip? What other channels will you use to tell your story?

### *#changehack 31 - animate your story*

In Chapter 8 on *Communicate to Co-create,* we explored the impact of communicating visually. Imagine the powerful combination of a story that is represented visually for your people to easily understand the key messages and remember them. New starters joining up to work on your project can watch it as part of their induction.

An effective way to communicate the story about your change initiative to your stakeholders, and more broadly across the organisation, is to animate your story. You can outsource this and have it completed in just a couple of weeks. Check out these two companies:

1 | *Sticky Stories:* They have an existing library of engaging stories about change management and leadership that you can subscribe to. Their list is growing so take a look at their website. They also customise stories for your change initiative.

2 | *Flimp Studios*: This organisation is very clever at creating change posters and animated videos that communicate key messages in an engaging way. You can watch samples of these clips on Flimp Studio's website, listed in my references.

### *#changehack 32 – curate your own stories*

- Establish a habit of observing and recording your own personal stories. What may seem like an ordinary experience has the potential to convey a rich message. These can be your customer experiences, employee experiences, personal, parental and family events.
- Practise retelling these stories with your colleagues and friends, using the Pixar framework.

- Draw on your collection of stories to find metaphors and links so you can re-purpose them to your current context.

### *Even more benefits*

Okay, so we know why stories are important as a change hack to improve engagement. There are numerous other benefits that you can share with your project team. Let them know that a well-structured story will:

- *Simplify your message, so others will understand it in plain English;*
- Make it easier for you to explain your project/change;
- Involve the project team to build the story, getting the project team on the 'same page';
- Provide a common language for your project team and stakeholders;
- Be depicted effectively on a visual management board.

### *TED talks can't be wrong*

If you've watched TED talks, you will have noticed some common characteristics of the more successful ones. Along with being engaging and genuine with an abundance of passion for their topic, each speaker is asked to include stories as anecdotes peppered through their delivery. When you read material on how to prepare and present a successful TED-style talk, you will find that most blogs and articles will recommend the inclusion of a story.

One blog, by Jenna Goudreau, explains the story as a 'hero's journey' which presents as a mini version of the Pixar formula. She recommends the hero's journey is presented in three parts: the call to action, the barriers to the achieving the end goal and the outcome or resolution. The hero's journey approach draws on information written by Jeremy Donovan, author of *How to deliver a TED talk: Secrets of the world's most inspiring presentations,* who said: *'From small meeting rooms to major boardrooms, storytelling is a becoming a bigger part of how people share ideas'.*

For too long, we've prepared our 'case for change' or 'project deliverables' in multi-page business cases and PowerPoint slide decks. I've joined many projects that had already kicked off, where it's taken a great deal of time to simply get across the key messages and purpose of the change. One of the greatest gifts we can give our project team and stakeholders is to help them simplify and convey their message in the form of a story, for optimal understanding and buy-in.

# 14 BEYOND THE STAKEHOLDER MATRIX

Decades before telephones and any other sophisticated communication technology existed, we relied on word-of-mouth to spread news, often by foot, horseback and more recently by sea and air travel. But not all news that travelled through these channels guaranteed that the message hit the mark. The communication channel is critical. But there is another key ingredient we often overlook when we plan our stakeholder engagement.

That ingredient can be found in this short history lesson. Let's imagine it is 1775 - the start of the American Revolution. Two revolutionaries, Paul Revere and William Dawes, set out on a horseback journey to spread the word to unite the country in the 'cause'. While Revere and Dawes covered the same distance and towns, with the same message, it was only Revere's that garnered the level of passion and support for the change.

In his book *The Tipping Point,* Malcolm Gladwell has identified Revere's approach and social presence as the ingredient that 'tipped' the message, and describes people with Revere's 'rare set of social gifts' as *connectors, mavens* and *salesmen.*

Now, about Paul Revere: he wasn't in a role that held positional power, such as a politician or community leader. He was a silversmith who was well connected and had great social presence. He belonged to numerous clubs representing diverse interests. He knew who to reach out to, in order to spread the message.

Does this sound like anyone you know in your organisation? Or perhaps it's you? It's the person who knows people in various pockets of the organisation, across business units and networks beyond the workplace, is trusted and extremely likeable.

When we look for our influencers, we often focus on stakeholders with formal, positional power. But this story reminds us that we also need to consider the hidden influencers. They may not have that formal power, by they do have social power and respect.

## CONVENTIONAL STAKEHOLDER MANAGEMENT

In change programs and projects, it's typical to see a great deal of effort applied to creating and updating stakeholder lists, or what has become known as the *stakeholder matrix.* We need to apply the same level of effort, if not more, to the conversations with our project team about the stakeholders, who will manage and own the relationships, the engagement priorities and finding the hidden influencers in the business.

A stakeholder is defined as a person or group in the business, or external party, who is impacted, and needs to be engaged in some way about the change. Engagement is varied: it can be to consult, advise, seek review, seek approval for decisions, or to inform. Stakeholders will perceive the change or event as either a gain or a loss. As we've seen from the Paul Revere story, when identifying stakeholders, it's not only the people who are directly involved in the change who need to be considered. There are usually additional key influencers in the organisation who may not have positional power and are not directly impacted by the change, but are valuable to involve or consult on the change due to their social influence.

The typical stakeholder matrix captures - more often than not in an Excel spreadsheet - a line-by-line record of each stakeholder, their role, division or business unit, contact details, communications channels and their level of interest or 'stake' in the change. The better ones record engagement activity, with a closer look at stakeholder challenges, opinions and influencers. And we know that effective stakeholder engagement is so much more than the matrix – we need to spend time with our project leadership team, together in one room, to discuss the challenges, the priorities and our next actions.

## THE ROLE OF CHANGE LEADERS AND PRACTITIONERS

One of the core capabilities of the change leader and practitioner is stakeholder management and engagement. This capability is defined as the ability to identify and engage stakeholder groups to build support, acceptance and ownership of the change. The change responsibility is typically to assist with the identification of stakeholders and to create and maintain the stakeholder matrix.

The change practitioner's role is to develop, in consultation with the project leadership team and/or senior sponsors, an engagement plan that considers:

- buy-in
- anticipated resistance and proposed interventions
- optimal channels and/or forums for face-to-face engagement, with identification of stakeholder communication preferences
- clear ownership of stakeholder relationship management, to avoid duplication
- strategies to build strong partnerships
- potential conflicting interest with other organisational events or related programs taking place

- relationships *between* stakeholders - can one stakeholder influence another?
- level of participation required from stakeholders.

There is a general consensus that stakeholder engagement is important. It's regarded as expertise that the change professional brings to the program. However, when carrying out a post-implementation review (PIR) or retrospective, it's often identified as one thing that many project teams wish they had done better.

## MATRIX ALTERNATIVES

There are several good models that take a mapping approach to stakeholders, which is more visual than a conventional matrix spreadsheet approach.

### *The conventional power/interest grid*

The power/interest grid is a popular framework to group stakeholders and prioritise engagement activity and effort.

Power is usually interpreted as *formal power*, which is easy to identify by organisational hierarchy, as it's based on position and title. Don't forget to include the hidden influencers here, who have information authority through social power.

The level of interest in the change may be difficult to measure at first. You may need to assess this with a change readiness assessment or short survey of your stakeholders. The best way to gauge interest is by asking people. For example, the employees who come along to your Lean Coffee session have demonstrated interest already.

Grouping stakeholders on a grid can be subjective and needs a discussion with the stakeholder relationship owners, who are usually members of the project team.

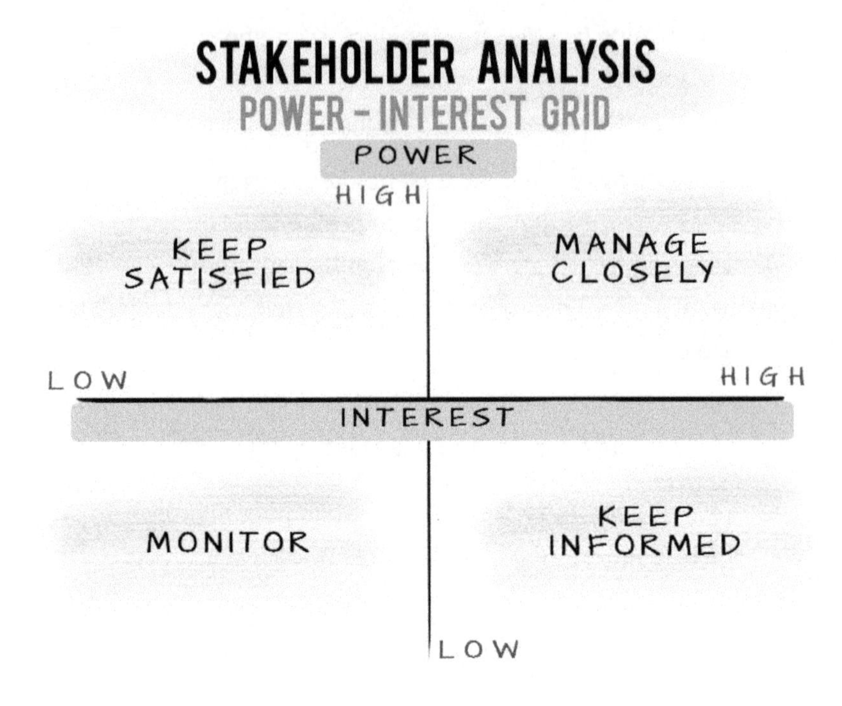


With each stakeholder group, change consultants typically identify engagement actions as a guideline, as shown in this table:

| **Keep satisfied**<br>***High Power, Low Interest***<br>**Latents**<br>• Engage and consult to find an area of interest, hot button<br>• Aim to increase level of interest | **Manage closely**<br>***High Power, High Interest***<br>**Promoters, key players who can *stop* or *delay* your project**<br>• Focus efforts on this group<br>• Involve in governance, decision making |
|---|---|
| **Monitor**<br>***Low Power, Low Interest***<br>**Apathetic**<br>• Keep in the loop with general newsletters, intranet updates<br>• Aim to move to High Interest, especially if they start to make noise | **Keep informed**<br>***Low Power, High Interest***<br>**Defenders who can be great *advocates* for your project**<br>• Show consideration, look for change champions to leverage the energy |

### *#changehack 33 - tweak your stakeholder grid for win/lose analysis*

Remember Chapter 11, *The Truth About Resistance*? Some businesses are now considering the dynamic of what stakeholders perceive to *win* or *lose* from the project or change, which plays directly with our hardwired response of moving towards reward (win) and running away from threat (loss).

I first introduced templates that take into account threat and reward responses in a white paper I wrote in 2014 (available on my website), titled *Navigating through transformation: A neuroscience-based toolkit for change.*

In this toolkit, I revised the stakeholder analysis grid which is inspired by David Rock's SCARF model of threat and reward, and applied this scenario as an example:

An organisation is planning to outsource its call centre. The Executive team will be rewarded with financial bonuses if cost-effectiveness is achieved within a short time frame. Some groups (business units) are affected more than others.

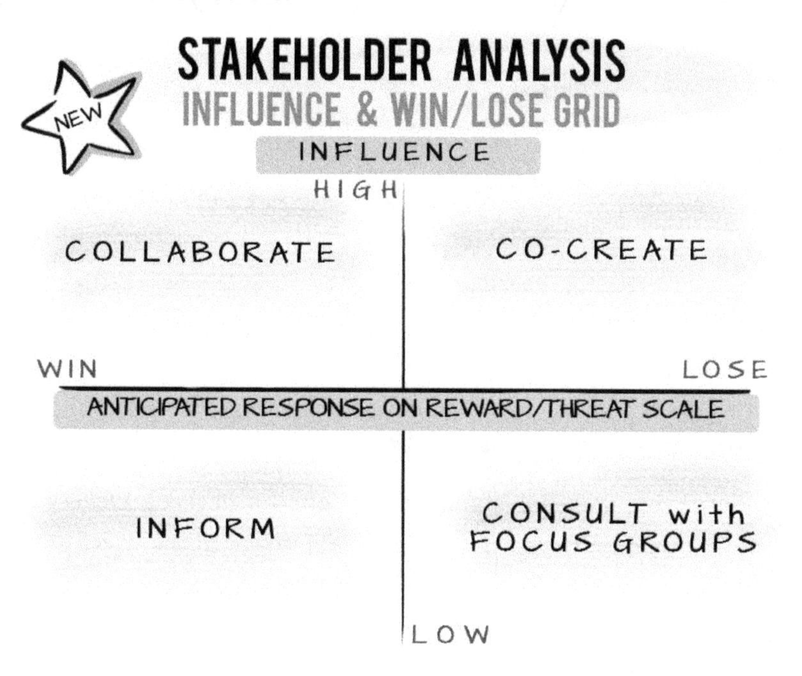

This table suggests activity for each quadrant, drawing on a couple of #changehacks explained in earlier chapters:

| **Collaborate**<br>***High Influence, Low Threat*** | **Co-create**<br>***High Influence, High Threat*** |
|---|---|
| Look for your advocates and change champions here. This group could benefit from a workshop on the SCARF self-assessment to help them understand the range of responses, and to build empathy towards their peers who may be experiencing a different response. | Promoters, key players who can **stop** or **delay** your project.<br>Focus efforts on this group by uncovering their pain points.<br>*See #changehack 24 from Chapter 11.*<br>Run a SCARF self-assessment workshop to open a discussion about emotions, and uncover the SCARF element triggers of status, certainty, autonomy, relatedness and fairness. This will help with the co-creation of solutions that can reduce the threat response. |
| **Inform**<br>***Low Influence, Low Threat*** | **Consult with focus groups**<br>***Low Influence, High Threat*** |
| With gains expected and low level of influence, this group will require minimal effort. Some in this group with social influence can be excellent advocates for the change. Another place to find your change champions. | Because these defenders can be great ***advocates*** for your project, actively consult them via focus groups and discussion forums.<br>*See #changehack 4 in Chapter 5* for more on involving users in Journey Map workshops. |

Have you noticed that the word *power* has been replaced with 'influence' in this version?

### *Where the real power or influence lies...*

When identifying stakeholders, we often look for decision makers and influencers based on their formal, positional power in the organisation. With that approach, it's easy to overlook employees who can be effective influencers with informal authority. We need to find our Paul Reveres.

The informal network is more social. This isn't just a social media network. A social network may include connections on Facebook, LinkedIn and Enterprise Social Networks, but in a workplace context, it means who you know well inside the organisation on a more personal basis.

Social networks are often established with a common ground outside work, through numerous channels such as sports clubs, school, postgraduate study, alumni, special interest groups, family and even book clubs. For example, a couple of years back, I was a parent at the same school where a couple of our Executive General Managers had children attending. We often socialise casually outside of the work setting when the sports teams have family events. These settings are opportunities to build relationships and trust outside the formal environment of work. It's often in these interactions that you can pick up critical information or clues as to what's either bothering or exciting the decision makers. We are all familiar with a story about business getting done quickly because Stakeholder A plays golf with Client X.

Regardless of how intricate the organisational design is in the workplace, informal networks will continue to exist. The key, and the hack, is to uncover the hidden influencers. The more conversations you have with your project team and colleagues about stakeholders, the more likely you are to uncover them.

Here are some tips on how:

### *#changehack 34 - see who's leading the way on your Enterprise Social Network (ESN)*

Who are the ones with a voice on your ESN? Who is bold, networking outside the conventional hierarchies and connecting effectively across silos? When I needed to launch the NED talks at work, it was the Yammer influencers who helped me drive the program through their support, reach and voice.

### *#changehack 35 - facilitate a project team session to discuss engagement*

The #changehack is to run a stakeholder engagement planning session, as a facilitated workshop, with your project leadership team. After the first one, most project teams will see the value in such discussions and will agree to participate in them regularly. If you go ahead with this hack, here's how:

#### *Principles to agree on with your project team*

- Confidentiality and discretion

Apply the 'what we say in this room about stakeholders stays in this room' rule. Carefully destroy any flipcharts that record comments about stakeholders. Remember to clean the whiteboard properly, especially the electronic ones that have rotating writing space. You'd be surprised (or probably not) at what I've seen when I've pressed the button to rotate the whiteboard in many a meeting room. Imagine how you would feel walking into a meeting room and seeing your name on a whiteboard, with little or no context?

- Frequency

You may agree to run these sessions quarterly, or for more agile teams, they may be needed monthly. Allow around 1.5 hours for each session.

The first session usually takes longer as you will need to outline the benefits and objectives, explain the process, the ground rules and what stakeholder commitment model you will apply. Allow 2 - 2.5 hours.

#### *Preparing for the session*

**1** | *Gather the inputs.* Meet with project team members to validate your stakeholder list. The business case often identifies a preliminary list as a start.

# STAKEHOLDER PLANNING SESSION

| INPUTS | OUTPUTS |
|---|---|
| ✓ Business case | ✓ Agreed information to update stakeholder map or matrix - e.g. stakeholder names, types and owners |
| ✓ Any risk assessments | ✓ Agreed TOP 3 engagement actions for each project team member for the next quarter |
| ✓ Existing lists or stakeholder matrix | ✓ Scheduled date for next planning session |
| ✓ Names from discussions with project leadership team members | |

2 | *Prepare the flipcharts for the walk-around brainstorm.* For each business unit or division, prepare a flipchart with the stakeholder names. The visibility of all names will help you kick off the discussion while participants walk around the room to look at each flipchart.

### *During the session*

- Agree on who are the influencers and decision makers, who will gain or lose, and who is the primary owner for each stakeholder;
- Each stakeholder owner identifies their top three engagement priorities for the next period, i.e. between now and the next session;
- Agree on key messages;
- Schedule the date for the next session.

### *After the session*

- Circulate actions for each stakeholder owner, as agreed, together with an invitation for next meeting;
- Update and circulate the stakeholder matrix;
- Find ways to keep the stakeholder discussion alive in project team meetings or at stand-up meetings; make it a regular agenda item by encouraging team members to speak about challenges, issues and wins.

### *Benefits of running the sessions – why bother?*

If you need to convince your project manager to put time aside for the team to attend this session, here are the benefits:

- Stakeholder issues and engagement priorities are visible to all members of the project team and are discussed openly;
- The project team can reach agreement on stakeholders in terms of engagement levels, by using a commitment curve or one of the grids discussed in this chapter - this provides valuable clues to engagement priorities and key messages;
- It brings the stakeholder matrix to life;
- It helps to identify the informal network from the formal hierarchy;
- All project team members have an opportunity to see the stakeholder map in real time and can offer support to each other in the relationship management;
- Transparency in the stakeholder approach means it's less likely that engagement and meetings will be duplicated.

### ***What about the matrix?***

This means that the stakeholder matrix, with its numerous updates, is simply an ***output*** of the rich and valuable discussions your project team will agree to schedule. In between these scheduled formal discussions, talk about your stakeholders more frequently in project team meetings.

As a regular agenda item, the project team will keep stakeholder relationships top of mind.

We know that effective stakeholder planning and engagement goes *beyond the stakeholder matrix.* As change practitioners, we can add a great deal of value in helping our project leadership teams, by facilitating a workshop or discussion to:

- identify stakeholder priorities;
- agree on key messages and communication channels;
- uncover the hidden influencers in the organisation and potential resistance (loss) and support (gains);

On a parting note - and back to the opening paragraphs in this chapter - who are the Paul Reveres in your organisation? Tap into their network, watch how they operate and learn from them. Don't just look for them - when you find them, identify what you can do to become your own version of Paul Revere!

## FACILITATION, NOT TRAINING

For anyone involved in influencing, leading or engaging others for change, it's great to have a few change hacks, like the ones we've discussed, up your sleeve. Developing facilitation skills is a valuable capability for managing and leading change.

People who deliver a great deal of training may be mistaken as facilitators. But facilitation is different to training. A trainer designs and delivers the content for the learner to achieve specific, pre-determined learning outcomes, for skills development. A trainer may deliver some of this content via facilitation, but they are two different skill sets. However, many trainers are also very good facilitators.

A facilitator guides a discussion to surface issues and help a group reach resolution or agreement on next steps. An expert facilitator helps their audience arrive at their own AHA moment – as we saw in Chapter 6 on *Mindset Hacks,* this is the time when a profound change in mindset can occur.

Facilitators are not necessarily subject matter experts; rather they are the experts in group process and human behaviour.

Facilitation is the skill that change practitioners and change leaders must learn to master. Apart from a lot of practice, or attending a formal training program on facilitation skills, here are some tips for you:

- Watch others facilitate. If you hear of someone running a session, ask if you can observe, or help with flipcharts or recording answers, so you can learn by observation. Make a note of the techniques you like and those you don't.
- Everyone has a style. When you watch others, you may see some techniques that you may not feel comfortable using straight away.
- Read as much as you can about facilitation. You may even find a facilitators' meet-up in your home town that you could connect with.
- Be familiar with the business environment in which you are operating. What are your organisation's strategic imperatives? Who are your main competitors? Who is likely to disrupt our business? What are the threats and the opportunities, the new markets and new entrants in the current market? What are our customer pain points? If relevant, I use this information to introduce the session upfront with a macro view of the business landscape.
- Become a curator. As soon as you see a prop, a quote or a story that could be used in a session, keep it. This will help you build your facilitator's toolkit of resources (covered later in this chapter).
- Use some well proven business models when needed. For example, in the rest of this chapter, the #changehacks draw on some of these that can be used in almost any business context.
- When collecting group ideas, pause to sum up key themes and ask participants to elaborate. Ask for examples if a point appears incomplete or needs further explanation. Then ask the group if any points need further clarification.

In an agile world, a strong facilitator is expected to run a session without a *slide deck* and without *answers*.

### *No slide deck*

This may sound scary at first, but it's not. In fact, it's liberating. I once spent hours preparing a slide deck for a facilitated session on stakeholder planning with a senior leadership team. I also had numerous flipcharts set up to frame their group discussions and contributions. On the day, the technology didn't work. While I tried to arrange another laptop computer, the project sponsor encouraged me to go ahead without the slide deck. At the end of the session, he told me that the session was better than he ever expected, because we had promoted more involvement by walking around working with the flipcharts.

Not only will it save you time; it will force you to hone your visual facilitation and flipcharting skills. You can whip up a simple agenda outline on flipchart paper and have another sheet ready for recording issues that need to be 'parked'. At the end of your sessions, take a photo with your phone (at least one person in the room will have a phone) and this could be all you need as your session record.

### *No answers*

Facilitators often venture into the land of the 'unknown unknowns'. Be clear about your role from the beginning; advise the group that you don't have all the answers and the purpose of the session is to uncover what they can, so they have all the issues out in the open.

Here are a few useful, existing models and frameworks you can add to your suite of facilitation techniques.

## USEFUL MODELS AND FRAMEWORKS

### *#changehack 36 – force field analysis*

A force field analysis, developed by Kurt Lewin, is a framework to gather feedback on the forces *for* and *against* a proposed change. With your project or change team, or any audience of change champions or coalition, brainstorm the positive forces that will drive or support the change, and the restraining forces that will present obstacles to the change. Then discuss how you can strengthen or leverage the positive forces and minimise or manage the obstacles. The discussion will provide a common understanding of the proposed change and potential resistance, clues on your change interventions or approach, and will uncover possible risks and issues to identify for your project.

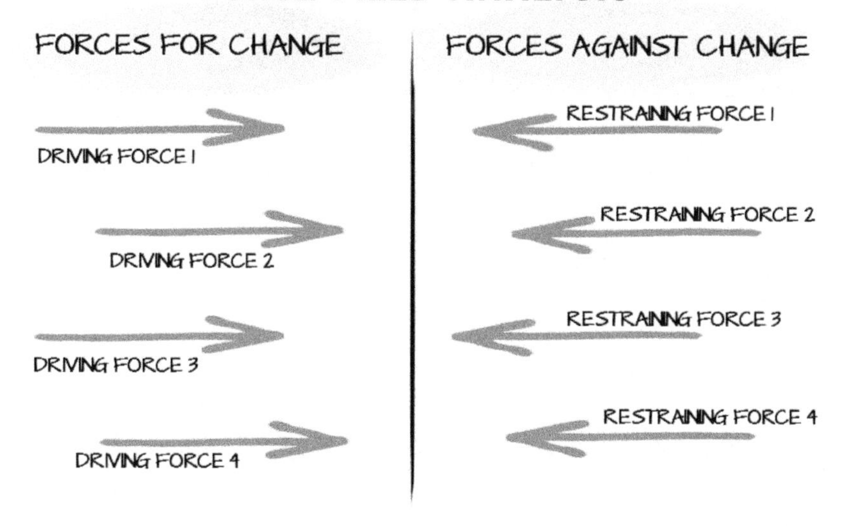


**SOURCE:** Framework developed by social psychologist, Kurt Lewin, in the 1950s.

### *#changehack 37 – 2x2 matrix*

The classic 2x2 matrix was introduced by the Boston Consulting Group in the early 1970s as the Product Portfolio Matrix to assess products for market share and growth. Since then, the matrix has proven to be a useful tool for problem-solving and prioritising.

I've used it to prioritise capability uplift activity, with one axis dedicated to effort required and the other axis for business return/value. This helped our team prioritise the training programs we would deliver, with a 'parking lot' for the lower value, 'nice to have' ones if we could secure more resources.

Here's an example with two axes, *cost* and *value*, that is often used:

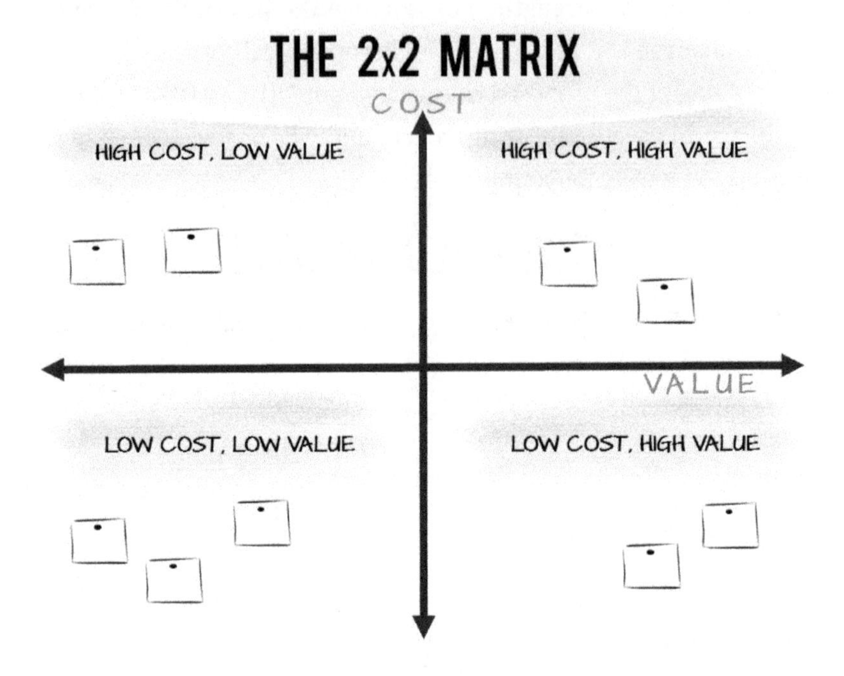


The *Will/Skill matrix* covered in Chapter 7 on *Agile Behaviours* is an example of how the 2x2 matrix is applied in a discipline outside marketing. In this context, the Will/Skill matrix helps you identify an approach for your people with high or low skill (capability) against their will, or desire to learn or complete the task.

## TECHNIQUES

### *#changehack 38 – fishbowl*

The fishbowl conversation technique is typically used in conferences that take an 'unconference' open-space conference approach. As a participant-centric meeting or discussion, the fishbowl dialogue can be set up with five to seven chairs arranged as an inner circle. Set up additional chairs in an outer circle or circles around this fishbowl or inner circle. The most participatory approach is to moderate an *open fishbowl* where one chair in the inner circle is empty, so any member of the audience can occupy the empty chair and join the fishbowl. Throughout the discussion, your participants come and go, so many can join in.

The advantage of this approach is that it hacks hierarchy, as the circle creates balance and equality. By inviting participants into the open fishbowl, you are providing opportunities for people to be heard, and their concerns are heard by the broader group, which fosters transparency. As the facilitator, you introduce the topic and ground rules, and act as moderator by setting a time limit on the session and the time the visitor stays in the fishbowl.

### #changehack 39 – walk-around brainstorm

There are various ways to generate ideas and stimulate creativity. One of my favourites is the *walk-around brainstorm*, sometimes called *carousel brainstorming*, as it maintains high energy levels in the room. If your workshop needs to gather ideas or feedback, try this technique.

Break up the group into three or four smaller groups. Arrange the room so you have the three to four flipchart stands or blank flipchart paper on the walls. For example, let's say you want to gather ideas with your project team on how to best engage three different stakeholder groups. Write the stakeholder group on each flipchart. Give each group a marker of a different colour. Advise your group that each smaller group has five minutes at one flipchart, and when you give them the sign that time's up, they will move to the next flipcharts, so they can review the previous group's contributions, add a tick if they agree with the existing comments, and add further suggestions.

As the facilitator, wrap up by reviewing the most voted suggestions and ask the group to agree on the suggestions they will own and implement.

An added bonus is that Stanford University researchers found that walking boosts your creativity!

#### *#changehack 40 - hacking an existing proposal*

Here's a common scenario I've facilitated often - a group session where a number of ideas have been recorded and I've needed to assess the popularity or viability of the ideas with a voting system where each participant leaves one, two or three circle shaped stickers to register their views. In this approach, you can see straight away which ideas have the group support.

There's another type you may be asked to facilitate, which needs a different approach. It's a session to guide the group to review, cull and reshape something already in draft, such as a proposed document, briefing pack, workshop content, or your project story. As someone who loves a little facilitation challenge, I've designed the ***HACK it™*** approach to tackle this.

The ***HACK it™*** approach works well because it provides four options for participants to table their view on the proposed document under review, and opens robust discussion where there are different views. The diagram is self-explanatory. Here's one way I've used it:

In designing a new #changehacks workshop for my clients, I invited them to a Discovery session, where I also applied the principles of Design Thinking. The purpose of Discovery was twofold. The first goal was to develop and agree on a change practitioner persona, who would feature in our case studies. The second - and key - goal was to walk through a proposed agenda for a two-day workshop I was in the process of developing. We used ***HACK it™*** for each proposed agenda item to gain insights on what we should:

- ***Hold***
- ***Add***
- ***Change***
- ***Knock out.***

At the end of the session, I was able to revise the session content based on the discussion and feedback. The Discovery participants attended my launch workshop and could see the outcome of their input and discussions in the revised session design. Co-creation at its best!

### *#changehack 41 – become a curator of the creative*

When you see something communicated or facilitated in a way that interests you, in and out of the workplace, collect it, take a photo or make a note. These ideas come via numerous channels. It could be an icebreaker activity a facilitator uses, a promotional brochure you find in your mailbox, or an idea you pick up in a blog or a tweet. If it grabs your attention and it's quirky in some way, chances are that it will have the same impact on your target audience.

### *You will see resources everywhere!*

It's just like when you buy a new car, and you suddenly notice that there are many other similar colours and models, just like yours, on the road. Once we develop an attachment to something, this selective attention occurs. This cognitive bias even has a name that you may never remember – the *Baader-Meinhof phenomenon*. Anyway, you want to create that same effect when you start hunting for ideas. Once you have your antennae tuned to those of a curator, you will find numerous gems to add to your repertoire.

### *Your reputation will precede you!*

Once you earn a reputation for being a great facilitator, you'll find requests for suggestions or perhaps be asked if you have time to run a session. It's flattering, of course, to be asked to help a group through an

## THE FACILITATOR'S TOOLKIT

Did I mention that the master facilitator is very well organised? It's great if you can have the following items at hand. At short notice, it can be challenging to find these materials, especially as more large organisations are carrying fewer stationery lines:

- Several packets of post-it notes, in different colours if possible
- A couple of rolls or pads of flipchart paper
- Adhesive tack
- Chunky markers – various colours for whiteboard, various colours for flipchart paper
- Your own icon library – that grows and grows
- Your library of activities – including these #changehacks, along with other ideas you've seen used for icebreakers, energisers, group/team dynamics, etc.
- Stress balls, coloured paper sheets, other props you can use for powerful, visual metaphors.

issue, challenge or to more clearly see options or potential solutions. And it's extremely rewarding to see the group reach their outcome. Because many requests come from outside your immediate team, I have one final tip here, to take some pressure off your workload - ask your 'requestor' to assign someone to help you. This helper can scribe for you and commit to compiling the post-session information for the group. You are there to facilitate the session. The team owns the post-session follow up and actions.

### *#changehack 42 – use the magic of metaphor*

Okay, since this is one of the final chapters, I really needed to stop with the tips and the #changehacks, but I did mention visual metaphors in the facilitator's toolkit. I thought I should give you a hint here on a couple that have worked for me:

#### 1. *Hoberman's Sphere*

This is a plastic, multi-coloured dome (named after its designer). It's ball-shaped and expands and contracts as the parts fold in and out with a scissor-like motion in the joints. It has been marketed as a toy, which means you can buy a couple quite cheaply. Google it and you will know straight away when you see it. I use it to demonstrate a closed or fixed mindset vs the possibilities of a learning mind that is open to new ideas.

#### 2. *Which shape is bigger?*

These are easy to cut out from coloured cardboard once you have a template that you can easily find on Google images.

I scatter a few pairs around on tables and ask participants to hold them up and ask each other – which is bigger? Clearly it's an illusion and they are both the same size. It opens up the discussion about how easy it is to think something is better, bigger or different at first glance, without exploring the reality.

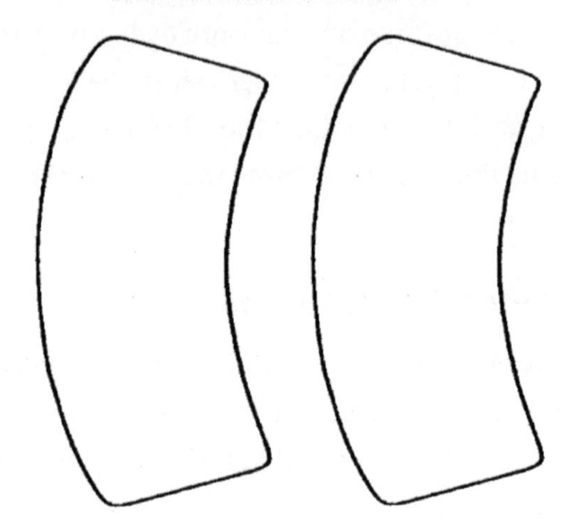


From now on, think about your facilitation style, how you can develop or fine-tune it and how you can use these techniques to help your teams hack for change!

# 16 MAKING IT HAPPEN

You've now read about the agile mindset, along with the behaviours and practices that go with it. Almost every chapter has a few change hacks for you to try out straight away, or park for the right time.

Some of you may be doing some deeper thinking about your role in getting other people on board, particularly with an agile mindset, behaviours and practices.

The best intended change plans can miss the element of *making the change stick.* Embedding the change to ensure it becomes part of the organisational DNA calls for some planning in itself. If we want to see agile change capability in the way our people lead and deliver change, we need to create an environment where the people receiving the change, often called *change receivers,* feel empowered to continually improve their business. These end users need to feel comfortable integrating agile approaches in their day-to-day practice.

## HOLISTIC VIEW

To create a shift, take a holistic approach that looks at three levels to truly make change stick:

1 | Organisational level

2 | Team level

3 | Individual level.

### *#changehack 43 - take a holistic approach for the shift*

At an *organisational level,* we know that it's the people who make up the organisation that contribute to organisational agility. It's when you have the critical mass - the right number of people at all levels with agile capabilities - that the organisation itself will become adaptive. It's at this level that we can introduce the organisational levers to reward and embed the agile behaviours and mindset.

At a *team level,* we have opportunities to make a difference, and bring agility, as a capability, to the forefront. This is where we can start our focus. Consider the mindset and capability of new team members, along with your existing team members. Do you have the right people on the bus? When recruiting new team members, what plans do you have in place to get the right ones on board?

At an *individual level*, start by asking yourself: *How can I make a difference in the workplace?*

We are now entering the realm of *culture hacks*.

What are you going to do? What can you do? What's in your sphere of influence? Many feel helpless and that they can't make a difference alone. But small things can make a big difference. Moreover, change leaders and practitioners are culture hacking all the time and may not realise it. We may miss opportunities to do even more, so let's explore four ways in which you can impact or make recommendations to shift mindset and behaviours - aka the culture!

## MAKING IT STICK

You can:

1 | ***Model*** what you want others to think, act and do

2 | ***Recruit*** the right people

3 | ***Reward*** the right mindset and behaviours

4 | ***Reinforce*** what you want to see repeated and embedded.

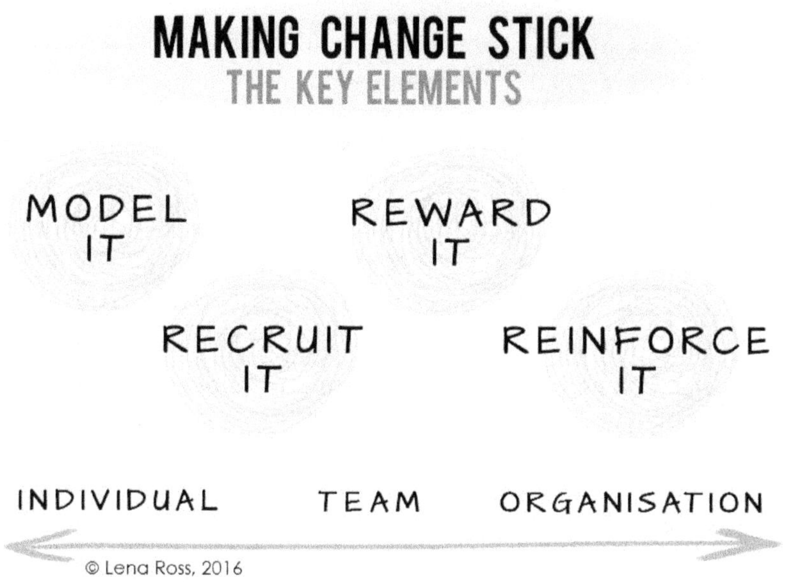

MAKING CHANGE STICK
THE KEY ELEMENTS

MODEL IT
REWARD IT
RECRUIT IT
REINFORCE IT

INDIVIDUAL
TEAM
ORGANISATION

© Lena Ross, 2016

### *1. #changehack 44 - model it*

Whether we have direct reports or not, we cannot underestimate the impact of our own behaviour on those around us. From the chapter on *Agile Behaviours,* we know that how we act is observed, absorbed and easily mimicked by others, making it critical that we model the desired behaviours.

This sounds straightforward, yet too often leaders miss this simple way of influencing others, and get it wrong. You would be surprised at what I've seen in my many years of working in and consulting to organisations. By way of just a couple of examples, I've seen the leader who:

- Advocates collaborative workspace/hot-desking practices while claiming a desk of their own;
- Communicates a rule that there are no mobile phones in meetings, yet they bring theirs because they are expecting an 'important' call;
- Consistently arrives late to meetings, and expresses impatience when waiting for others;
- Speaks to team members with little or no eye contact, while looking around the room or looking elsewhere.

I'm sure you have numerous examples to add to this list.

The *'do as I say, not what I do'* approach is too prevalent.

If you are in a leadership role, *status signals* like these communicate arrogance and will earn you little or no respect, while you demotivate your team. We are probably all guilty of doing things we are not particularly proud of, consciously or unconsciously, as part of our learning. The key message here is to be mindful of your actions.

Keep in mind that we are always modelling behaviours - consciously and unconsciously - and the people around us will copy us at a subconscious level. The ripple effect and emotional contagion of how we act has a significant impact on what others will do.

### 2. #changehack 45 - recruit the right people

Refer back to Chapter 7 on *Agile Behaviours,* where the Will/Skill matrix was discussed. In this chapter, we looked at the individual and team characteristics of the agile team, and the importance of having the right people on board for this team to work effectively.

To quickly recap on this theme, the Will/Skill matrix is based on the assumption that a skill is easier to teach than shifting an undesirable behaviour or low motivation. Keep this in mind when you recruit, and consider developing your selection approach on this model.

If you need to call in selection expertise, reach out to your recruiter or Human Resources business partner to develop a recruitment approach to source the right people for your team. You will need a clear definition of the required behaviours (that you can borrow from Chapter 7) so an appropriate search process and set of interview questions are established to attract and find the right talent. Ideally you will search and find the behaviours and capabilities you need.

Previous experience alone is not a reliable indicator. If a candidate has worked on an 'agile team' before, it's not a guarantee they have the mindset and behaviours you want. To help you identify the people you want on your team, the interview questions you ask need to uncover the alignment.

A couple of questions to get you started could sound like this:

- What did you like most about the last project you worked on?
- Tell me about a challenge you experienced when working with the team? And what you did about it?

Use the behavioural interviewing approach to hear about real examples where your potential team members can describe the situation, what they actually did and the outcome. To gather more information, probe a little further and ask:

- Then what happened?
- What did you learn from that?

### 3. #changehack 46 - reward it

One organisation I worked in invested a great deal of time and money developing their new 'corporate values'. Cascading from those values was a statement of the behaviours they wanted to cultivate. Out rolled the roadshow to spread the word, along with glossy, colour posters and business-card size pocket cards so we could all have them at our fingertips. How successful was this approach? Did the behaviours change? Did the change stick?

Sadly, no it didn't. One very simple element was overlooked. The behaviours where not clearly defined. There were no rewards for demonstrating them, or consequences for *not* demonstrating them. As a disclaimer, I must mention that this occurred in the days before I was a change practitioner, but I did ask why we were not being measured and rewarded on something that appeared to be important to the organisation.

Once you have identified the actions that demonstrate the mindset and behaviours you want to see, to support organisational agility, define them clearly. You may need examples to make the definitions easy to understand. Examples could range from exemplary behaviours to those less desired, to showcase the contrast of what is good and what is not so good.

These definitions need to be part of the organisation's reward and performance program, and to appear as desired behaviours in employee performance scorecards and capability statements. Once they land in the performance program, you can reward what you want to see.

*A word of caution here - if you want to embed a culture of agile thinking, where a beginner's mindset is critical, be careful that you don't 'punish' innovative thinkers who try something that doesn't work. Remember to praise the experiment, even if you need to have a conversation about the approach or the outcomes.*

### 4. #changehack 47 - reinforce and embed it

Okay, you have the first three ticked off. You are modelling the right behaviours, you have your recruitment approach aligned to get the right people on the bus, and your organisation's performance program is set up to reward the teams and individuals who are on board and demonstrating agile capability.

There is one more element to cover off - to see the desired behaviours repeated and embedded, so they become 'the way we do things around here'.

To reinforce is to repeatedly remind your people what you like to see in your organisation. You can use a few different approaches to get the message across:

- Make examples of great behaviour public through stories that appear on the corporate intranet;
- Encourage people to nominate team members they see doing the right thing, with a reward system in place for the nominees;
- Set up a Kudos Board for your own team, where team members can post notes on who they've seen demonstrate exemplary behaviour and what they did. How cool is it to see your own name in a public place when you least expect it?

*Another word of caution here - make sure you are publicly recognising those who really deserve it. Are you overlooking the quieter achievers? Otherwise, you run the risk of people experiencing threat if there is perceived unfairness in the allocation of rewards. Remember the SCARF model discussed in Chapter 11 on The Truth About Resistance.*

**Embedding** the right stuff is a result of repeatedly *modelling* it, *recruiting* it and *rewarding* it.

## FOR SPECIFIC CHANGE INITIATIVES

The hacks explained in this chapter are designed to embed agile change capability at all levels of the organisation. There are take-aways here for how you can ensure the change sticks for your own change initiative.

Think about your change plan for an initiative. A typical scenario in an organisation is one where the change has been delivered and the dedicated change practitioner is quickly rolled off that initiative. If the practitioner is an external contractor, they are likely to finish up and leave the organisation to pick up their next gig. If the person is an internal employee, they're often moved on to their next project to ensure they are fully utilised.

So who is around to make sure the change is handed over effectively to the change receivers? Who makes sure the change sticks?

### *#changehack 48 - identify measures through a human-centred lens*

In your change plan, check that you have identified the indicators in the 'future state' that demonstrate success. In the spirit of co-creation, I apply a human-centred journey map approach to identify practical measures: I ask those who are impacted what they think success looks like in the future state, by visualising what they will be doing, thinking, and feeling when the change is implemented.

This is shown in the following diagram, based on an infographic titled 'making change stick' which I designed and can be downloaded from my website. Of course, the list of measures shown in this diagram is an indicator only, and they will vary depending on the type of change you are introducing.

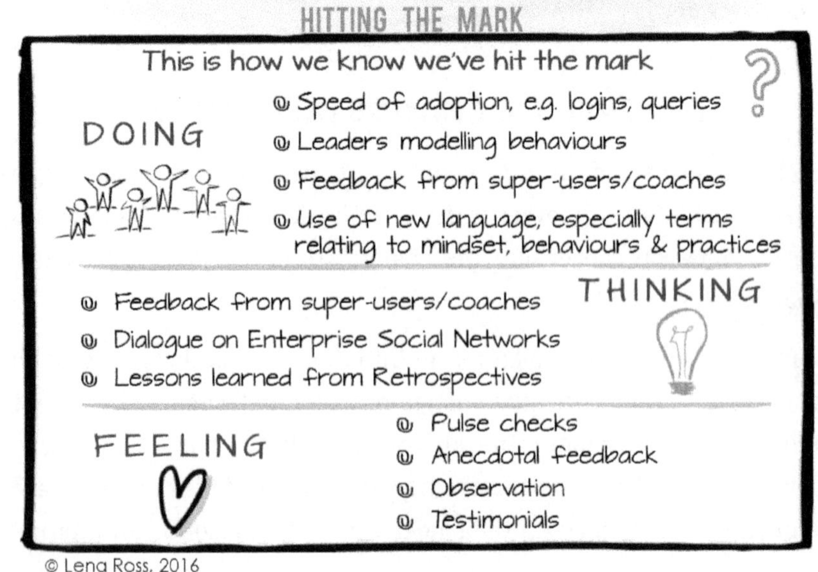

To reshape the culture in your organisation, you need to introduce processes and measures to shift the way your people think, behave and work as individuals and in teams.

I'll wrap up this chapter with one of my favourite quotes, often attributed to Peter Drucker:

***What is important is measured,***
***What is measured is done,***
***What is done is rewarded,***
***What is rewarded is repeated.***

This is where the rubber really hits the ground. Sounds like a good change management approach to me!

## STAYING ABREAST OF IT ALL

An interview question you are likely to hear more frequently - or should hear more often - is: *How do you stay abreast of industry trends?*

As information evolves so quickly, we know that books and blogs alone will not provide all the answers. This means that we will learn fast, we'll make mistakes, we'll learn as we go, from each other and by connecting, to keep our knowledge and skills relevant.

I ask this question when interviewing for change consultants because it provides an insight into the candidate's mindset, the level of their appetite for self-directed learning, and level of curiosity. By understanding how they grow professionally and personally, outside formal learning channels provided for them, I can understand their degree of comfort with social media and networking outside the organisation. It provides a good sense of their capability *and* motivation to bring an outside-in view to their practice.

If you're not already a lifelong learner, now is the time to jump on board. In the VUCA environment, learning is less likely to be provided for you in the traditional face-to-face forum. Welcome to the era of self-directed learning. Lifelong learning is a necessary practice, not only to stay abreast of what's happening, but also to achieve mastery in your chosen field.

If you want to future-proof your value, either as an employee or independent consultant, self-directed learning is critical. It's likely a great deal of that learning will be through informal channels. There is even a cool word for a person who is self-taught, outside the typical classroom or educational channels - it's an *autodidact!*

## LEARNING IS FOR LIFE

Lifelong learning is for everyone - even for Jogoro Kano, who founded the martial art practice of judo. As Kano was approaching his final days, he asks his students to bury him in a white belt, which denotes a beginner. Most of his students were confused that their esteemed teacher and master would ask such a thing. But the wiser students understood the symbolism of his request – that their teacher was entering his new life as a novice, ready to learn again. Here the message of lifelong learning is clear: regardless of how educated or experienced we are, there is something yet to learn.

### *Get in the driver's seat*

Focus on what you ***can*** do. Social media and access to online learning and networks have made it easier than ever before to stay ahead of the curve in your field. We know that organisations are spending less on formal training budgets, particularly as more permanent employees are being replaced by contractors. This places a greater importance on directing your learning through developing your ***Personal Learning Network*** (PLN), to navigate disruptive times and to continue to grow.

Developing a PLN signals an intention to learn, with an understanding that much of this learning will take place organically. This type of mindfulness applied to your learning will enhance all your capability types

- for *match fitness, business fitness* and *evolutionary fitness* - covered in Chapter 3.

### *Now... a couple of hacks for your personal growth!*

### *#changehack 49 - develop your Personal Learning Network (PLN)*

#### *Why you need your own learning network*

A Personal Learning Network is your informal (outside a classroom and books) learning network, where you learn from various sources and through numerous channels. By connecting with a range of people, you will tap into different perspectives, fresh insights, and as in any curious journey, you will discover the unexpected. You probably already have a form of PLN; however, it's worth working on it, to expand your reach.

A PLN is based on the principle of 'paying it forward', which means that you may not always 'repay' the person or source who helped you, but you share your learning with someone else. The added benefit is that when you help others learn, you learn more. You will recognise this concept from an earlier chapter, as 'teaching to learn', which is based on the assumption that you are motivated to learn more about your topic when you are sharing your knowledge with others.

The concept of learning through a vast network ties in neatly with how we are hardwired to connect and learn, as seen in Chapter 10, as *Hardwired for Social*. This type of learning has been hailed as the way to learn in the 21st century.

Your knowledge and learning is greatly enriched through face-to-face interaction *and* social networking. My first-hand experience of connecting with industry peers within and outside my own country, through LinkedIn and Twitter, has certainly exceeded my expectations. The generous sharing of knowledge and support I've received from leading, well-respected practitioners such as Jason Little, Dr Jen Frahm, Gail Severini and Paul Thoresen, particularly through social media, has played a significant role in my learning journey and building my confidence to keep on blogging, and to write this book.

When I work with groups and individuals to help them scope their network, we follow this process:

1 | Brainstorm as many channels as we can that will offer learning through networking. Keep in mind that these are also opportunities for you to share your expertise and knowledge – it's two-way!

2 | Draw your own PLN as a concentric circle map, with at least three areas:

- ***Inner circle*** – your immediate network, workplace team and/or family;
- ***Middle circle*** – your workplace or professional network outside your immediate team;
- ***Outer circle*** – everything else, covering Twitter, LinkedIn, TED talks, Hangouts, Meet Ups, Blogs, Webinars, Podcasts, Conferences, MOOCs (Massive Open Online Courses), events.

3 | Review it regularly and refresh. It will grow. You will soon notice that less of your learning is taking place in a formal classroom and more of it is happening through social connection and networking.

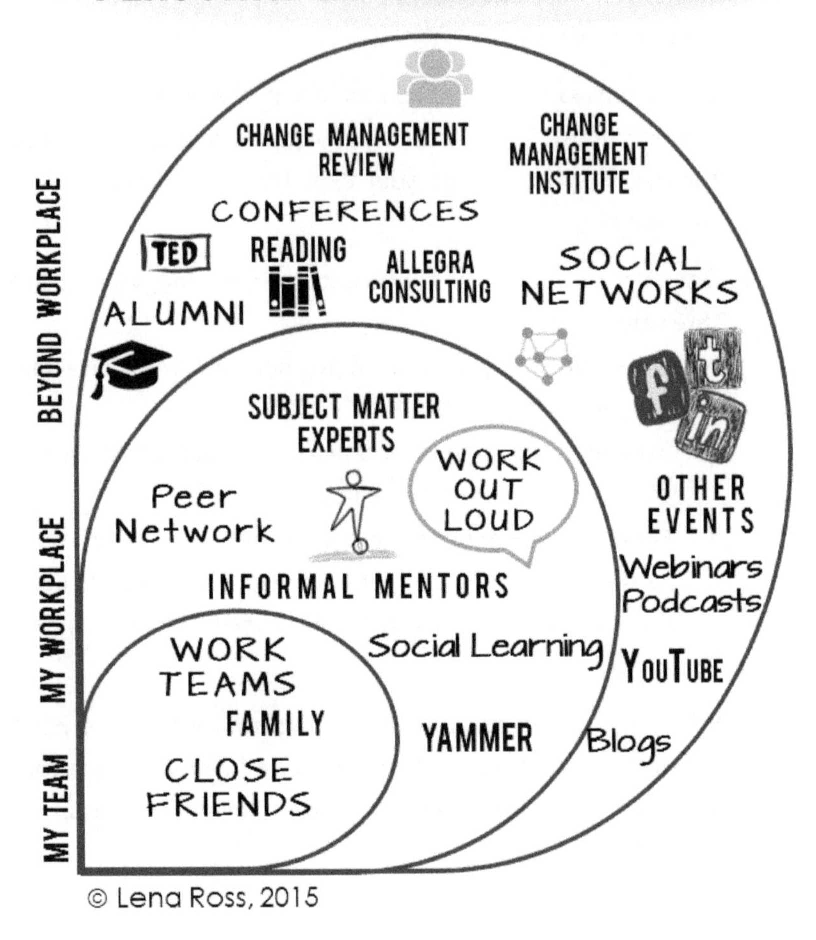


### *#changehack 50 - get the most out of conferences and networking events*

Conferences provide an ideal social learning environment. In the one forum you get the latest thinking in your field, most of which isn't even published in books yet. The agenda is carefully planned to bring you the latest and best. It's the modern version of a clan gathering where the intersection of networking and learning takes place in an environment of focus and commitment. People have suspended their day-to-day activity in pursuit of social connection and information in a non-hierarchical forum.

Here are my three hot tips on how to enhance your experience and learning at these events:

### *Think global*

Look beyond your own city and country. There are conferences in all fields all over the globe, and it's worth considering the option of combining a holiday with a conference. My Australian change management colleagues who have made the trek across the oceans to attend offshore events have not been disappointed. They have come back with ideas, insight and rave reviews. It will have an amazing multiplier effect on your network.

### *The thought leaders are everywhere: on AND off the stage*

Network with everyone. You will meet as many interesting people off the stage as the ones who are presenting. If you are active on social media, you'll meet people you're already connected with and add so many more. It's a meeting of the minds and you can bet that the delegates who've made the effort to attend such an event are as committed as you and will have an interesting spin on how they can apply the information.

### *Get onto social media in real time*

Enhance your post-conference connections by 'back-channelling' during the conference. Back-channelling means you share your key learnings on social media (usually Twitter), ideally with photos, while you are at the event. By sharing learning, participants extend your own experience as you pick up on what others have taken away as key points. Most conferences have a dedicated hashtag to use in posts, so you can easily search online afterwards.

## *#changehack 51 - become intensely curious*

In Chapter 4, *Agile Mindset Mastery*, we looked at curiosity as a critical element in developing an agile mindset, despite its being associated with punitive consequences, such as killing a cat. But now it's cool to be curious.

It seems everyone is talking about how important this attribute is for leaders, entrepreneurs, intrapreneurs... in fact, everyone. Where would we be without our natural curiosity? In our history as humans, it's been the more inquisitive among us who have challenged the status quo, made breakthroughs, discovered other continents and invented new technologies.

There are some very good reasons to be more curious, that surely make it a quality we all need:

### 1. *It opens new networks*

What have you learned by simply talking to people, asking questions and being interested in their work, hobbies or family? By cultivating an interest in people, you will find out more about your customers and their preferences, and make connections with a broader network. CPA CEO, Alex Malley, recently blogged how being curious about people and having the courage to engage in unlikely places - such as on flights or at children's sporting events - has opened unexpected new networks for him.

### 2. *Your brain will love it*

Our brains are hardwired to file and recall new experiences. When you continue to learn, you build new neural pathways, keeping your mind active and agile. Discovery is exciting and the curious brain is rewarded with new information, such as when you have an 'aha' moment, where you get that insight, or epiphany. Neuroscientist David Rock explains that when we solve a problem through a flash of inspiration, our brains enjoy a burst of dopamine, the feel-good chemical associated with the 'reward centre' in our brain.

### *3. It helps you deal with ambiguity*

Being continuously open to learning and new ideas means we search and find more clues and facts. These become anchors of certainty in an increasingly disruptive complex and ambiguous environment, helping us break new ground. Discovery of information that helps solve even small parts of a problem leads to a deeper knowledge over time, making us better at managing complexity and more tolerant of ambiguity. In our search for new ideas, we remain nimble and can more easily change tack when the winds take a different direction.

### *4. It suspends judgement*

Curiosity helps us practise the art of the fifth of Stephen Covey's famous seven habits - *Seek first to understand, then to be understood.* By investigating facts and searching for further data, we detach ourselves from the need to be right and work towards a state of understanding new possibilities. Nance Guilmartin, in her book 'The power of pause', has labelled this discipline *Get Curious Not Furious,* a process that allows us to pause and investigate before responding too early with bias or emotion.

### *5. It develops a growth mindset, driving social learning*

The more curious you are, the more opportunities you'll explore proactively to learn socially and organically. Your personal learning network (PLN) will have no end, as represented in my curiosity matrix below. A curious mind, hungry for new information, is the key attribute of a growth mindset. A growth mindset, as opposed to a fixed one, is one that thrives on challenges, and welcomes failure as an opportunity to learn and improve.

## ***The curiosity matrix – which quadrant are you in?***

In the spirit of applying one of my favourite facilitation hacks described in Chapter 15, I developed the curiosity matrix as a 2x2 matrix to represent the relationship between your appetite for curiosity and the span of your

PLN. The more curious you are, the more opportunities you will enjoy to learn socially and organically. The infinity symbol ∞ reminds us that curiosity and learning have no end!

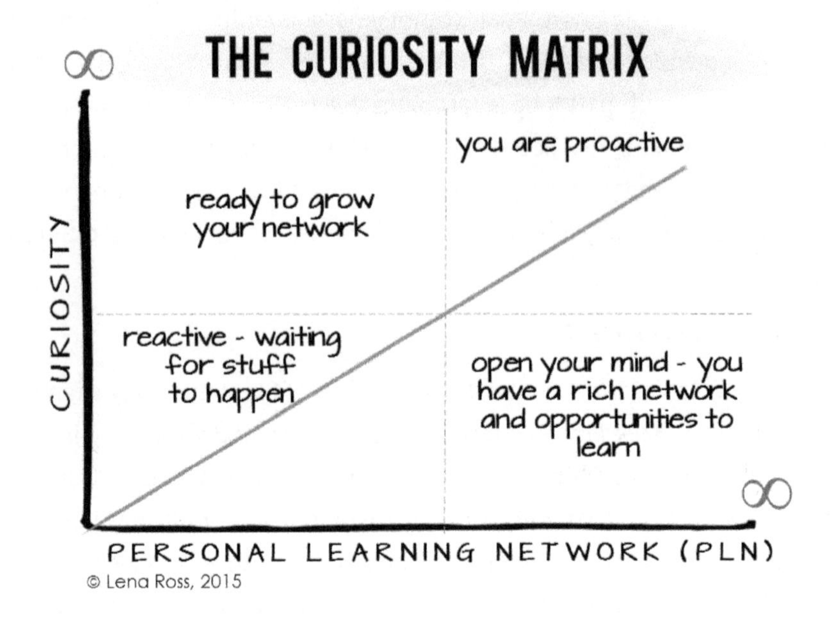


A healthy dose of curiosity is what you need to remain nimble and to develop and grow your PLN. Curiosity, with your PLN, is the path to self-directed and social learning so you can learn quickly, just-in-time, what you need to know in a disruptive world, where change is the new normal.

Ask yourself regularly:

*When was the last time I learned something for the first time?*

## WHERE WILL CHANGE MANAGEMENT LAND?

Now that change is no longer a process, are we still 'managing' change? How relevant is the term, activity or role title of 'change manager'? Are we really managing change, or designing human-centred approaches to ease adoption and deliver rapid solutions?

Are we becoming change navigators or transformation consultants? This book doesn't intend to address this, but it does ask the question and provoke the thinking. Our roles are being transformed, as are the capabilities expected of us.

Traditional change management practice has given birth to terms such as 'change fatigue' and 'change readiness' as activities or considerations for successful change. But now that change is the new normal, a business that doesn't have the inbuilt capability, or cannot restructure its organisational DNA to absorb ongoing change, will no longer have a competitive advantage. One possibility is that the 'change readiness survey' will be an artefact of the past and will give way to a 'change agility quotient'.

Regardless of where the nature of our role actually lands, there is a compelling need to self-direct our ongoing learning, develop our Personal Learning Networks, gather as many hacks as we can, and challenge ourselves to demonstrate agility in this disruptive, complex world.

## ON YOUR MARK...

You now have #changehacks under your belt, and are ready to go!

As you've seen, it's not a step-by-step approach, but rather, a handy set of tips you can use to hack for change in dynamic business environment. Organisations are expected to respond to market demands faster. In turn, change and project practitioners will be expected to know and apply ways to achieve cut-through in the workplace of the future. Your #changehacks, your curiosity and your evolutionary fitness will keep you ahead of the pack.

Happy change hacking!

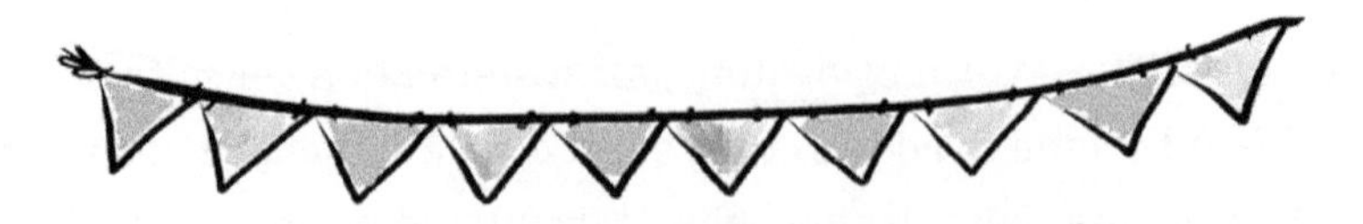

The more that you read,
the more things you'll know.
The more that you learn,
the more places you'll go!

Dr Seuss

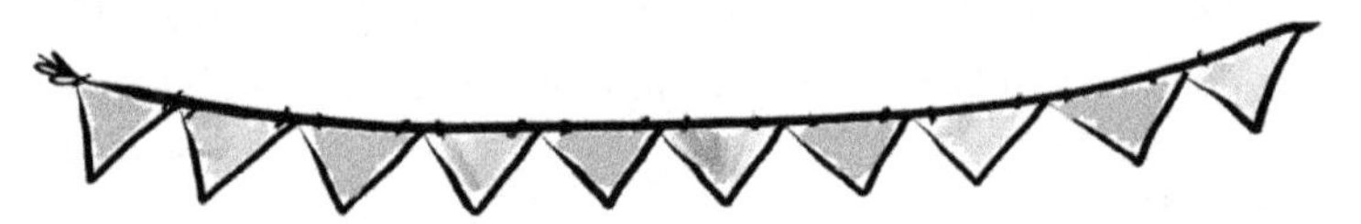

Before we recap all the hacks, consider this: have you ever used the *Kanban* approach for your own to-do list? It's a great visual way to see your work flow. I used my own Kanban on a wall poster with sticky notes to manage and monitor my work progress when writing this very book.

### *#changehack 52 - your personal KANBAN*

Now that you've read the book, and know more about over 50 change hacks, you're not going to just put it away on your bookshelf. Remember, small things make a big difference, so here's a tool to help you keep the hacks top of mind.

Use the template on the next page to record the hacks you want to try out, or have tried out, so you can keep track of what a great change hacker you are!

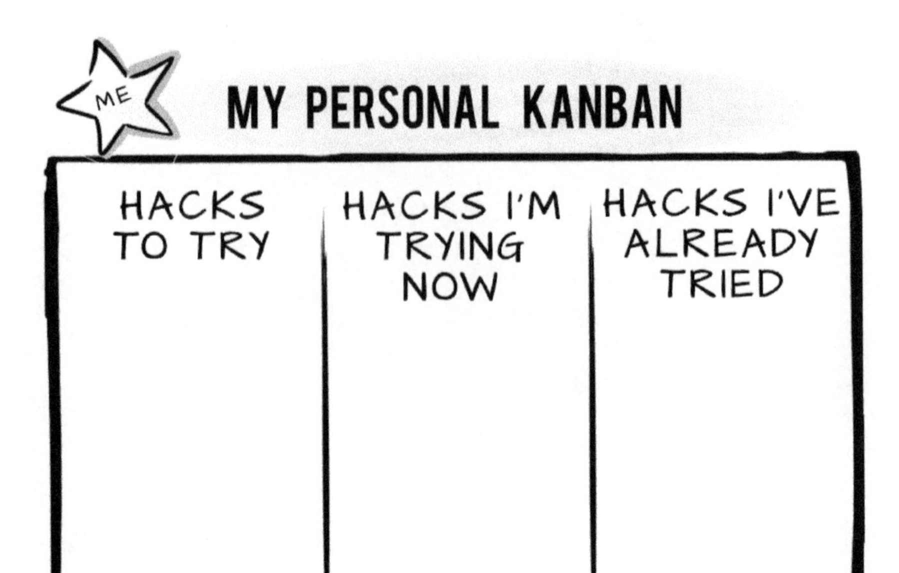


***Share your thoughts***

- What are your favourite #changehacks?
- How have you used them?
- What response did you get?
- Have you tried any new ones?

I'd love to know, and I'm sure our fellow change hackers will be interested too.

Let us know via 'social' in your tweets, and your Facebook and LinkedIn posts. In the spirit of hacking, tag me in your posts so I can respond ☺

It's a small world! You can find me and connect on:

www.facebook.com/changehacks

www.linkedin.com/in/lenaross

@LenaEmelyRoss

### *The HACK of all hacks...*

As promised, here's a summary table of all the #changehacks, by chapter:

#### Part One: How you think

| | Chapter | Hacks |
|---|---|---|
| **4** | Agile mindset mastery | #1 - Listen to your self-talk |
| | | #2 - Think like a beginner |
| **5** | Thinking by design | #3 - Develop personas of your end users |
| | | #4 - Run a journey workshop |
| | | #5 - Cook up an idea storm |
| | | #6 - Show the future state in a journey map |
| **6** | Mindset hacks | #7 - Schedule me-time |
| | | #8 - Create an AHA environment |
| | | #9- Power up your playlist |

**Part Two: How you act**

| | | |
|---|---|---|
| **7** | Agile behaviours | #10 - Get the right people on board |
| **8** | Communicate to co-create | #11 - Use your Enterprise Social Network as a change communication channel<br>#12 - Get your people on board with Enterprise Social Networks<br>#13 - Invest in a one-day course on visual facilitation<br>#14 - Try working out loud |
| **9** | How we are wired to behave | #15 - Consider Dunbar's number in organisational restructures<br>#16 - Chunk communication so it can be digested<br>#17 - Tap into grapevines<br>#18 - Tap into the power of rituals and ceremonies |
| **10** | Hardwired for social | #19 - Remind people that we learn when we want to and need to<br>#20 - Unleash your internal talent for social learning<br>#21 - Share what you learn with others<br>#22 - Send one person to attend a course or conference with the intent to share<br>#23 - Encourage team members to run a project spotlight session |
| **11** | The truth about resistance | #24 - Run a team self-assessment session<br>#25 - Gather tips to reduce the threat response |

**Part Three: What you do and deliver**

| | | |
|---|---|---|
| **12** | Agile practices | #26 - Host a think-ubator<br>#27 - Get on to gamification<br>#28 - Run a retrospective<br>#29 - Run a future-spective for your team |

| | | |
|---|---|---|
| **13** | Tell the story | #30 - Help your project team build the story<br>#31 - Animate your story<br>#32 - Curate your own stories |
| **14** | Beyond the stakeholder matrix | #33 - Tweak your stakeholder grid for win/lose analysis<br>#34 - See who's leading the way on your Enterprise Social Network (ESN)<br>#35 - Facilitate a project team session to discuss engagement |
| **15** | Facilitation hacks | #36 - Use a force-field analysis<br>#37 - Use the 2x2 matrix<br>#38 - Apply the fishbowl technique<br>#39 - Facilitate a walk-around brainstorm<br>#40 - Hack an existing proposal<br>#41 - Become a curator of the creative<br>#42 - Use the magic of metaphor |
| **16** | Making it happen | #43 - Take a holistic approach for the shift<br>#44 - Model the behaviours you want to see<br>#45 - Recruit the right people<br>#46 - Reward the right behaviours<br>#47 - Reinforce and embed<br>#48 - Identify measures through a human-centred lens |
| **17** | So what, now what? | #49 - Develop your Personal Learning Network<br>#50 - Get the most out of conferences and networking events<br>#51 - Become intensely curious |
| **18** | Recapping the hacks | #52 - Set up your personal Kanban |

# REFERENCES

*More info and interesting stuff...*

There are so many great resources out there to build your Personal Learning Network (PLN) and continue learning. Here's the information I've referred to in this book:

## IN THIS BOOK

### *Preface*

Highlights from the Australian Institute of Training and Development Awards Night 2015 - found on my YouTube channel, link on www.lenaross.com.au.

### *Chapter 1*

Gartrell, A. (2017), 'Robo shock: the jobs automation will pinch', *The Melbourne Age,* 17 April 2017.

Millennials in the workplace by 2030 - from a blog in www.forbes.com titled: '*Millennials in the workplace: they don't need trophies but want reinforcement*' (2015).

### *Chapter 2*

Find the Agile Manifesto, values and principles on www.agilemanifesto.org.

### Chapter 3

Lawrence, K. (2013), *Developing leaders in a VUCA environment,* UNC Kenan-Flagler Business School, White Paper.

My own white paper of emerging capabilities for change mastery found on my website, titled: *High 5 of change mastery* (2016).

### Chapter 4

Dweck, C. S. (2006), *Mindset: The new psychology of success*, Ballantine Books, New York.

Guilmartin, N. (2009), *The power of pause: How to be more effective in a demanding 24/7 world,* Jossey-Bass, San Francisco.

Chamorro-Premuzic, T. (2014), 'Curiosity is as important as intelligence', *Harvard Business Review* (online blog) – accessed 20 June 2015.

Rock, D. & Schwartz, J. (2006), *The neuroscience of leadership*, Strategy and Business, No. 43, pp.1-10.

### Chapter 5

Brown, T. (2009), *Change by design: How design thinking transforms organizations and inspires innovation,* Harper Collins, New York.

Stanford Institute of Design, d.school, (2012), *Bootcamp Bootleg* - PDF toolkit resource available online on their website www.dschool.stanford.edu.

www.ideo.com

www.frogdesign.com

### Chapter 6

Doidge, N. (2007), *The brain that changes itself: Stories of personal triumph from the frontiers of brain science,* Viking Press, New York.

Ross, L. (2000), 'Baroque Power - using music to stimulate whole brain learning', *Australian Institute of Training and Development,* Vol.27, No.5, pp.23-24.

Rose, C. (1985), *Accelerated learning,* Accelerated Learning Systems, Buckinghamshire.

### Chapter 7

Blogs by Esther Derby can be found on her website www.estherderby.com.

Blogs by Christian Miles can be found on www.christianleemiles.blogspot.com.au.

TED Talk by Jeremy Heimans, '*What new power looks like*', 2014 on www.ted.com.

Landsberg, M. (1996), *The tao of coaching: Boost your effectiveness at work by inspiring and developing those around you,* Profile Books, London.

### Chapter 8

Stepper, J. (2015), *Working out loud: For a better career and life,* John Stepper self-published.

Medina, J. (2008), *Brain rules: 12 principles for surviving and thriving at work, home and school,* Pear Press, Seattle.

Websites for infographic templates:

https://www.canva.com/

https://piktochart.com/

### Chapter 9

Johnson, M. (2005), *Family, village, tribe: The story of Flight Centre Limited,* Random House, Sydney.

### Chapter 10

Leiberman, M. D. (2013), *Social: Why our brains are wired to connect*, Random House, New York.

Dr Jen Frahm's website - look for #SHOC with Bronte Jackson where Bronte talks about rituals in the workplace, posted on 10 July 2016, found at www.conversationsofchange.com.au/water-cooler/.

Information on the cascading mentoring program and the protégé effect http://ideas.time.com/2011/11/30/the-protege-effect/.

### Chapter 11

Rock, D. & Schwartz, J. (2006), The neuroscience of leadership, *Strategy & Business,* No. 43, pp.1-10.

Rock, D. (2009), 'Managing with the brain in mind', *Strategy & Business* Autumn No. 56, pp.1-10.

My own white paper on the neuroscience of change, found on my website, titled: '*Navigating through transformation: A neuroscience-based toolkit for change',* (2014).

### Chapter 12

www.benlinders.com Ben is an agile coach who has written a lot about retrospectives and future-spectives.

### Chapter 13

Dumb ways to die produced by Metro Trains, Melbourne - link to YouTube https://www.youtube.com/watch?v=IJNR2EpS0jw.

Pixar's rules of storytelling, originally formulated by Emma Coats, can be found on http://pixar-animation.weebly.com/pixars-rules.html.

Sticky Stories, where you can view trailers and free samples of their library http://www.stickystories.co/.

Flimp Studios and examples of animated change management clips can be found on www.flimpstudios.com.

Jenna Goudreau's blog: '7 Pubic Speaking Secrets from the most popular TED talks', November 2013, *Business Insider Australia,* accessed January 2017 https://www.businessinsider.com.au/public-speaking-secrets-from-popular-ted-talks-2013-11?r=US&IR=T.

TED Talk by Uri Hasson, '*This is your brain on communication*', 2016 on www.ted.com.

Donovan, J. (2012), *How to deliver a Ted talk: Secrets of the world's most inspiring presentations*, Self-Published.

### Chapter 14

Gladwell, M. (2000), *The tipping point: How little things can make a big difference,* Little, Brown and Company.

My own white paper on the neuroscience of change, found on my website, titled: '*Navigating through transformation: A neuroscience-based toolkit for change*', (2014).

### Chapter 15

Kurt Lewin's Force Field Analysis.

Boston Consulting Group - 2x2 matrix.

### Chapter 16

Landsberg, M. (1996), *The tao of coaching: Boost your effectiveness at work by inspiring and developing those around you*, Profile Books, London.

### Chapter 17

Covey, S. (1989), *The 7 habits of highly effective people*, Simon & Schuster, New York.

Alex Malley - Follow Alex on LinkedIn and you will easily find his blogs.

## WEB RESOURCES

www.agilemanifesto.org.

www.benlinders.com - Ben is an agile coach who has written a lot about retrospectives and future-spectives. He has presentations on SlideShare too.

http://www.changemanagementreview.com/ - A great site featuring podcasts, events around the globe and articles. Sign up for their weekly newsletter.

www.conversationsofchange.com.au - with Dr Jen Frahm, look for blogs. We need to talk about Agile, and her recommended bloggers and tweeps, and her famous podcasts are a must to listen to!

Dumb ways to die - on YouTube
https://www.youtube.com/watch?v=IJNR2EpS0jw.

## GET CURIOUS WITH MORE

*Web resources*

www.allegraconsulting.com.au

Allegra Consulting is a Melbourne based company specialising in change management recruitment, consulting, coaching along with a suite of educational events to build change capability and change agility.

www.lenaross.com.au

There are plenty of free resources on my website - white papers, info-graphics, blogs and YouTube clips that include my lightning talks on various change management topics.

*#brainpickers*

Watch #brainpickers episodes on the dedicated YouTube channel #brain-pickers. You can also find the #brainpickers link on my website.

### *Explore free online courses*

There is a list of free online courses at https://www.mooc-list.com/.

Courses from top universities at Coursera - https://www.coursera.org/.

And edx at https://www.edx.org/.

### *Interests*

Facilitation - check out the International Association of Facilitators (IAF) on https://www.iaf-world.org/site/.

### *Industry Association websites*

https://www.change-management-institute.com/australia.

# GLOSSARY

## *The lingo...*

### *Used in this book*

| Lingo, acronyms and abbreviations | What it means... |
|---|---|
| Agile - big A | Refers to the agile values and principles outlined in the Agile Manifesto, for Agile Software Development. |
| agile - little a | The broader use of the word agile as a word, to describe someone who is nimble or quick, ie behaviours and mindset that is agile, outside the context of Agile Software Development. |
| Agile Manifesto | Also called the Manifesto for Agile software development, lists four key values and 12 principles to guide an iterative and human-centric approach to software development. |
| Alpha state | A state of relaxed alertness, with a brain wave pattern of nine to 12 cycles per second. |
| Avatar | A representation of a person, usually in the form of an icon. |
| Baader-Meinhof phenomenon | When you come across new information or an item, and then you start to notice it appearing frequently. |
| Behavioural economics | A branch of economics that draws on insights from human behaviour to explain buyer/consumer decision making. |
| Bodystorming | A technique used in Design Thinking where a role play is carried out as if the product or service is developed, ie imagining the future state. |
| Change initiator | The person in the organisation who has decided to introduce the change. |

| Lingo, acronyms and abbreviations | What it means... |
|---|---|
| Emotional contagion | The process where a person influences another through their behaviour and actions, either consciously or unconsciously. |
| Change receiver | The person who is on the receiving end of the change, often required to adopt new behaviours and/or ways of working. |
| CQ | Curiosity Quotient - the level that an individual is motivated to be a self-managed learner. |
| Customer centricity | A way of doing business that is focused on a positive customer experience. |
| Design Thinking | An approach that uncovers multiple possibilities before creating a desired solution for customers and/or end users. |
| Dunbar's number | The number of people (150) with whom we are cognitively designed to maintain a social network. |
| Ecole mutuelle | The French term that translates to 'mutual school'. A social and collaborative learning approach where older students teach the younger ones. |
| Empathy map | A design thinking tool to gain deeper insights into our customer segments or users. |
| ESN | Enterprise Social Network, such as Yammer, Slack. |
| FOW | Future of work. |
| Future-spective | Like a retrospective, but asks the team to take a future-forward view by imagining the sprint/project has been completed. |
| Gamification | The application of game design to another activity such as learning, or to encourage engagement with a new product or service. |
| HCD | Human-Centred Design. |
| Journey map | A design thinking tool that uncovers the customer's interaction with the product or service at various touchpoints, highlighting potential pain points and opportunities for improvement. |

| Lingo, acronyms and abbreviations | What it means... |
|---|---|
| Kanban board | A visual representation (such as a board) of work in progress; what work has started, been completed and yet to commence. |
| Lagom | The Swedish word that means 'not too much, not too little, just right'. |
| Lean Coffee | A structured meeting where the agenda is decided by the participants. |
| Lightning talk | A short presentation, five to 15 minutes in duration. |
| MOOC | Massive Open Online Course. |
| MVP | Minimum Viable Product. A deliverable (product or service) that contains sufficient features to deliver value and/or objectives, often to seek user feedback for further refinement. |
| Neuroscience | The study of brain activity and its impact on behaviour. |
| Pecha kucha | The Japanese word for a very short presentation with a prescribed format of 20 slides that are shown for 20 seconds each, with the total presentation taking 6.40 minutes. |
| Persona | A composite character that represents characteristics, such as demographic and psychographic, of a customer segment or user group. |
| PLN | Personal Learning Network |
| Pixar Framework | A six-step storytelling framework developed by Pixar Films, that you can use to structure the story of your change initiative. |
| Product owner | Your key stakeholder, aka project 'sponsor'. |
| Retrospective | At the end of each iteration, the retrospective, also known as the 'retro', is carried out for the team to reflect on what happened and what can be done differently in the next iteration. |
| SCARF | A framework that shows how our brains are hard-wired to sort events into threat or reward, based on five elements that make up the acronym SCARF - status, certainty, autonomy, relatedness and fairness. |

| Lingo, acronyms and abbreviations | What it means... |
|---|---|
| Scrum master | The facilitator for an agile development team, aka project/program manager. |
| VM | Visual Management. |
| VUCA | Volatility, Uncertainty, Complexity, Ambiguity. |
| Wagile | A convergence of the two words 'waterfall' and 'agile' where a project is applying agile practices in a largely waterfall framework. |
| Waterfall | A waterfall project follows a linear, sequential process that is not iterative. One stage is typically completed before the next one begins. |
| WOL | Working Out Loud. |

### *Other relevant and useful terms*

Not exhaustive, but here are some other commonly used terms, particularly in the ***big A*** Agile world:

| Lingo | What it means... |
|---|---|
| Burn down chart | A graphical representation of what work is left to do vs time remaining. Used to predict when planned work will be completed. |
| Definition of done | The agile team determines what 'done' means, as a list of criteria, in the context of their project. |
| Epic | Work which is expected to take a full sprint to complete. |
| Jira | JIRA software is an agile project management tool, to plan, track and manage agile software development. |
| Product Backlog | A list of activities or tasks that need to be completed. |
| Scrum | The iterative and incremental software development framework that manages product development. The SCRUM framework is designed for teams to self-organise and make changes quickly. |
| SDLC | Software Development Life Cycle - a characteristic of waterfall project methodology, |
| Showcase | An informal meeting where the iteration/sprint outcome is reviewed. The outcome showcases, in the form of a demo, the completed features to the product owner. |

| Lingo | What it means... |
|---|---|
| Sprint | A repeatable and regular work cycle, also known as an iteration. A sprint varies in duration, often from one to two weeks to 30 days. |
| Timebox | An agreed time frame assigned to an activity. You will hear this used as a verb, eg 'let's timebox this'. |
| T-shirt sizing | A method to estimate using relative sizing rather than absolute sizing. Estimation is often used to size backlog items. |
| User Story | A feature or requirement that can be estimated and tested. A user story is assigned a value in points from 1-5 for estimation purposes, called 'story points'. |
| Velocity | Estimates how quickly work can be completed in a timebox period. Calculated by multiplying story points by the number of stories. Eg if the team completes 10 stories worth two story points each, the team's velocity is 20 story points per sprint. |

## ACKNOWLEDGEMENTS

Whilst I'm the author of this book, we know that we don't fly solo.

I am part of a family, village and tribe.

***Tribe...***I wouldn't have been able to compile my experiences, insights and learnings without the wonderful people around me in the workplace, and in my professional network, who granted me permission, and endless patience, to experiment, brainstorm, to hack, and to try again...and again. You trusted some of my off-beat ideas along with some conventional thinking, and we pulled most of it off and broke some new ground in the areas of change leadership and practice.

***Village...***Thank you to my colleagues and peers who encouraged me to put all this together because they believed I had something valuable to share.

In this *village*, I found my reviewers, my book cover designers and my profile picture photographer. So, a big thank you to reviewers Dan Paulet, Jo Wilson and Stacy Payne, who took the time to read my final drafts and challenged me to revise and fine-tune with their candid feedback and comments; the Monash University Art, Design & Architecture Faculty (aka MADA) students who designed my book cover after intense design briefs - Amelia Lazarus, Jonathan Vu, Alana Nanasca and Sigitjaka Nakula - and their supportive lecturers, Dr Cameron Rose and Dr Gene Bawden, who allowed me to be their 'live client'; and to my good friend and colleague, Joanne Rinaldi, who is an exceptional change practitioner *as well as* a talented photographer, and took a set of profile snaps that capture the real me!

***Family...*** Of course, I'd like to thank my amazingly tolerant family members, who also reviewed, challenged and poked me to revise and polish. A special mention of course to my 'other half', Grant, an excellent coach and video producer, who nudged me to the finish line, interrupting me only to record another #changehacks lightning talk or #brainpickers episode with Dr Jen Frahm. It was Grant's research and knowledge on our hardwired biases that helped me shape the information about our primal instincts.

And of course my two adult offspring, Anthony and Justine, who will be rewarded with exquisite karma.

## ABOUT THE AUTHOR

Lena Ross is an experienced and mildly disruptive change consultant with a reputation for valuable content creation and speaking at conferences and events.

Since establishing her consulting practice #changehacks in 2016, Lena been invited to share her expertise as a guest blogger and podcaster on the future of change management and emerging capabilities.

Lena's work draws on the latest thinking in change management from areas such as agile approaches, design thinking, future of work, digital and hardwired human behaviour.

Her future-forward views and approaches to collaborative learning, disruptive communication channels, and human-centred applications to delivering change are all designed for deep engagement and co-creation.

With Dr Jen Frahm, from Conversations of Change, she set up the #brainpickers YouTube channel, where they talk about hot topics in change management, with tips for leaders and change practitioners.

Her experience is well complemented by her relevant tertiary qualifications, such as a Master of Business Administration (MBA) from Monash University. This means she is able to apply sound academic discipline to the development of practical and innovative solutions.

Lena's services include onsite consulting, workshop facilitation, coaching and speaking.

Born and bred in Melbourne, Australia, Lena is often spotted balancing the city life with the serene energy of Daylesford, in the beautiful spa region of Victoria, Australia.

To find out more about Lena's work and her resources, visit her website on www.lenaross.com.au

Lightning Source UK Ltd.
Milton Keynes UK
UKHW020649100820
367987UK00019B/2151